# ACROSS THE SEAS

# ACROSS THE SEAS

*A.A. Gill Started It All - A Memoir*

by

## Elizabeth Sharland

A Passion for people and places

Including destinations in the author's life:
London, Paris, New York, Toronto and Palm Beach.

Including a Memoir

# ACROSS THE SEAS
## A.A. GILL STARTED IT ALL - A MEMOIR

*iUniverse books may be ordered through booksellers or by contacting:*

*iUniverse*
*1663 Liberty Drive*
*Bloomington, IN 47403*
*www.iuniverse.com*
*1-800-Authors (1-800-288-4677)*

*Because of the dynamic nature of the Internet, any web addresses or links contained in this book may have changed since publication and may no longer be valid. The views expressed in this work are solely those of the author and do not necessarily reflect the views of the publisher, and the publisher hereby disclaims any responsibility for them.*

*Any people depicted in stock imagery provided by Thinkstock are models, and such images are being used for illustrative purposes only. Certain stock imagery © Thinkstock.*

*ISBN: 978-1-4917-9407-4 (sc)*
*ISBN: 978-1-4917-9409-8 (hc)*
*ISBN: 978-1-4917-9408-1 (e)*

*Library of Congress Control Number: 2016905452*

*Print information available on the last page.*

*iUniverse rev. date: 05/03/2016*

**Other Books by Elizabeth Sharland:**

*Passionate Pilgrimages…from Chopin to Coward*

*Love From Shakespeare to Coward*

*From Shakespeare to Coward*

*The British on Broadway*

*A Theatrical Feast of London*

*A Theatrical Feast of New York*

*A Theatrical Feast of Paris*

*The Best Actress (Novel)*

*Blue Harbour Revisited…a Gift from Noel Coward (Novel)*

*On The Riviera (Novel)*

*Classical Destinations*

*Waiting for Coward (Play)*

*www.sharland.com*

In praise of *Passionate Pilgrimages...From Chopin to Coward:*

*Elizabeth Sharland will squire you to places you never thought you'd go, in impeccable language and with rare grace. Learn, then, how George Sand whiled away the hours with Chopin at Chateau de Nohant, and spent some time with Somerset Maugham at Cap Ferrat near Nice. Katherine Mansfield charms us in Menton, Italy, Cole Porter in Paris, Paul Bowles in Morocco and Lady Gregory in Ireland. The illustrations are lavish, offering visual clues to the geniuses that inhabit these pages. Travel with Sharland as you have never traveled before. A blessing on your Cranium.*

*MALACHY McCOURT*

*Elizabeth is a musician, artist, pianist, a traveler, and a playwright... who better to guide us on these journeys?*

*HUGO VICKERS The Unexpurgated Beaton:*
*The Cecil Beaton Diaries*

In praise of *A Theatrical Feast...Sugar and Spice in London's Theatreland*

*ISBN 0-9531930-2-0*

*Elizabeth's Theatrical Feast lives up to its title. This book is practical enough to tempt the appetite of the hungry diner, and crammed with titbits of historical interest with which to tantalise the imagination of the fascinated reader.*

*CLAIRE BLOOM*

Dedicated to Colman Jones

# Contents

## PART ONE

# PART TWO

A.A. Gill Started It All

## A MEMOIR

# Acknowledgments

A.A.GILL, ED VICTOR, COLMAN JONES, John Money, Sandy Paul, Anthony Bond, Ruth Allen, James Spiers, David Lerner, Robert Spencer, Pamela Hall, Ken Starrett of the Noel Coward Society, David Webster, and all my friends at Cunard. Thank you for your help.

The reason this book is part travel, part memoir is because the hotels featured in this book were the inspiration for my other books on travel. Also the Savoy Hotel gave me my first book launch party. Writers usually have their heroes, or for want of a better word, someone who they admired and inspired them to write and in some cases, travel. For me, it was Somerset Maugham, Noel Coward, the Bloomsbury Group, including Virginia Woolf and her wonderful work A Room of One's Own, with the evocative atmosphere of a truly unique place to stay. Instead of describing these hotels in my memoir (Part Two), I decided to place them separately in Part One.

## *Introduction*

STAYING AT AN OLD HOTEL is infinitely more interesting and enjoyable if you know something of the history of the establishment and more particularly, who stayed there. Even a novel set in the hotel is interesting: the thought that you might recognize a character in the hallway or someone who looked like them. Many novelists have written novels or short stories based in hotels, real or imaginary, such as E.M. Forster's *A Room with a View* or Thomas Mann's *Death in Venice,* and many by Agatha Christie; Scott Fitzgerald begins his novel *Tender is the Night* at the *Hotel Eden Roc* on Cap D'Antibes, in the south of France.

Hotels stand like grandfather clocks, ticking away the time from generation to generation. They have been featured in so many people's lives. A wedding, a honeymoon, an unforgettable holiday, some more tragic, crimes and misdemeanors, all give a hotel unique history and patina. I am always curious if I find a grandfather clock in a hotel: what stories they could tell.

When visiting the Italian Lake District some years ago, I felt a prickling up and down my spine, when entering a hotel on Lake Como. My grandmother and a maiden aunt, long since dead, had been on a Grand Tour in Italy sometime in the 1920s and we knew that they had visited Lake Como. Crossing the lobby, a grand marble staircase facing me, I felt their presence strongly; it happened again in the gracious old dining room that evening, and the next morning, walking down the front steps. Unexplainable, but I felt their spirits there. It would be interesting to know from others if this has happened to them. I wished that I had the old suitcase back at home, belonging to them, because there were some old hotel labels still stuck on them from the hotels where they had stayed.

All the following hotels have history. The facts are given to you in their brochures; sometimes they offer the name of the original owner, or the architect, but not very often, especially on their websites. Nowadays they offer great photos and videos of their rooms and spas and restaurants instead, but not much history.

Noel Coward based one of his plays at the *Beau Rivage Palace* in Lausanne and he also wrote short stories and letters when he was staying there on innumerable visits. Dirk Bogarde lived very near the *Colombe D'Or Hotel* and Restaurant in St. Paul de Vence, it was one of his very favourite places. He loved living in the south of France and after the publication of his letters, a huge volume skillfully edited by John Coldstream, it is interesting to read about his life in those surroundings. He used to take many of his house guests to lunch at the *Colombe D'Or* and he writes about falling in love with Simone Signoret even before he met her beside the swimming pool one summer afternoon.

My first novel, *The Best Actress,* tells the story of Nicole, a British actress who loses the love of her life on the night she wins the Oscar, and the sequel, *Blue Harbour Revisited,* describes her later trip to visit Noel Coward's house in Jamaica. This story is part of a third novel about Nicole *On the Riviera* when she returns to Cannes with a new project to discover where the romantic writers of the 20th Century lived and worked, including Graham Greene, Scott Fitzgerald, Cyril Connolly, Somerset Maugham and Katherine Mansfield.

# Chapter One

# HOTEL BEAU RIVAGE, LAUSANNE SWITZERLAND

ARRIVING BY TRAIN FROM GENEVA, Lausanne is situated on the very large Lake Leman and this hotel is a mile or two downhill from the railway station.

It is advertised as the *Beau Rivage Palace* and indeed the whole building is rather like a palace, with its own private driveway leading up to the impressive entrance.

As you can imagine, the hotel has a magnificent classical dining room, which is one of the most sensational in Europe. There are two other restaurants. You can have breakfast outside on the picturesque patio overlooking the lake. The breakfast alone will keep you going all day. It is a feast: dishes ranging from caviar, smoked salmon, kippers, to all kinds of omelets and egg dishes made to order, as well as what the British call a "good fry-up." Plus about two dozen kinds of pastries, croissants, bread rolls, cheeses from the region, fruits and yogurts. The dinner menu is slightly different in each restaurant and there is a Head Chef for each room.

The hotel is made up of two hotels. In 1864 an extension was begun and in 1908 a magnificent rotunda added which is now the dining room. It is not until you see the hotel from the front gardens that you can see where they join up, but inside there is no difference. The architecture is the same: the main corridor runs through the whole hotel. It is a hotel full of history.

In 1898 Empress Elisabeth of Austria was staying at the hotel incognito, when she left to take the ferry to Geneva. Walking along the promenade with a friend, she was assassinated, dying shortly afterwards back at the hotel. She had been stabbed by a crazed man who was later caught, but he had plunged a knife into her bodice, which was so tight that it was another hour or so before it was discovered it had been a mortal blow. By that time it was too late to save her.

On July 14th 1923 the Treaty of Lausanne was signed in the hotel's magnificent dining room. The treaty settled the conflict between the Ottoman Empire and the British Empire, as well as the French Republic, Italy Japan and Greece. The original treaty was in French because it was the second time an attempt for peace was made after the failed Treaty at Sevres, which had been signed by all the previous parties but rejected by the Turkish National Movement. However this Treaty of Lausanne defined the borders of the modern Turkish Republic. In the treaty Turkey gave up all claims to the remainder of the Ottoman Empire.

My main interest in staying there was because Noel Coward stayed there when a young man and he reported in his diary what he wrote there. He would take a picnic, packed by the hotel, in a boat out on the lake, after writing in the morning. He often used to take the ferry in the evening to Evian in France, where there was a casino. Evidently he won quite frequently, and he said once, when he was on a winning streak, they held the last ferry for him.

He was a friend of the writer Somerset Maugham and Coward wrote a play called *Suite in Three Keys* which is based at the hotel. The script consists of three short plays and it is a well-known fact that one of the characters is based on Maugham. Maugham also wrote in his diary about staying there and enjoyed playing Bridge with other guests during his stay. Famous guests of the past included Victor Hugo, Coco Chanel, Saint-Saens, Sacha Guitry, Gary Cooper and more recently, Phil Collins.

The lakeside suites and room with balconies on the lakeside are the best for the view. The French Alps in the background, with the lake and the little sail boats in front. Old fashioned steamers glide by on their way up to Vevey or Montreux and it is very pleasant to spend the day sailing up the lake, having lunch or dinner on board. Charlie Chaplin lived just outside Vevey and you can see the house as the ferry draws into the dock. Each town has its celebrities.

We took the ferry one morning to Montreux, home of the famous Jazz Festival each year. We then took a tiny train, which climbs up the mountain behind the city, sometimes going through steep tunnels in the rock, to arrive at a village called Glion. The train stops there before continuing on to several other stops, until it reaches the top of the mountain, with its tremendous view of the valley below. We stopped at the famous old *Victoria Hotel* at Glion where many of Coward's friends stayed when they came to visit him at Chateau Coward, just a view miles away in the village of Les Avants where Dame Joan Sutherland was a neighbour. I searched and found the little English Cemetery in Glion where both Coward's companions are buried side by side, Cole Lesley and more recently, Graham Payn. The view from their grave sites is breathtaking, overlooking the whole valley below.

The little train station is very old and takes you back to Victorian times. You can take a cable car which is next to the train station; it goes straight down like a lift, as you can see the cable line descending in a straight line. We chose to take the more leisurely train back down to Montreux. As you sail back to Lausanne, the *Beau Rivage Hotel* sign is painted across the front of the hotel, as in earlier times, as seen in the old brochures. The hotel has its own steamer and has dinner cruises on the lake, especially enjoyable when there is a full moon. The atmosphere is so peaceful and old fashioned: it reminds you of the days when travelers did the Grand Tour of Europe, staying at these elegant hotels. Porters would stick their hotel labels on your luggage as you left. I still have an old suitcase belonging to my grandmother with some of those old labels still attached. It is a marvelous place to visit when you are next in Europe.

# Chapter Two

# SAVOY HOTEL
# THE STRAND, LONDON

IT IS NOW TEN YEARS since the *Savoy* was renovated and totally restored to its former majesty.

The Savoy Grill is back in place, as is the River Room, now named the Kaspar dining room, and the celebrated Front Lobby. All the rooms and suites have been made new again. It is always interesting to describe the menus and the décor but this hotel is so unique because of its long history, the huge number of famous guests, the list of historical events that happened here, that I would like to write about these fascinating facts.

In 1884, the construction of the *Savoy* began using the profits of the *Savoy Theatre* next door. The artist James Whistler sketched the scaffolding, returning in May 1896 to stay at the hotel. His series of inspired etchings made from his Savoyards window captured the essence of London at the close of that century.

Claude Monet's passion for the Thames led him to paint it in all-weather conditions and times of day—but almost always from the same vantage point—his room on the fifth floor of the *Savoy*. When the light changed, he would put one canvas aside and turn his attention to another, and so on as the day advanced. He stayed at the hotel on three occasions between 1899 and 1901. His painting of Waterloo Bridge painted from the hotel in 1900 is now in Dublin.

Just before leaving for South Africa, early in 1898, businessman Joel Wolff gave a dinner party for 14 at the hotel. One guest cancelled at the last minute but the host balked at the superstition that whoever left the table earliest would be destined to die first. A few weeks later, Wolff was shot dead in his office in Johannesburg. Since then, if there happened to be 13 guests at a party, a member of staff would be recruited to join them. This, however, was not always convenient or practical, so Kaspar the Cat was commissioned by the Savoy from art-deco designer Basil Ionides in 1926. His brief was to design a three foot-high cat, which he carved from a single piece of plane tree.

Christened Kaspar, he now lives on a high shelf in the Pianoforte Room, with his back to a mirror and is only removed if a party of thirteen is lunching or dining at the Savoy. He is then placed on the fourteenth chair with a napkin before him, changed as he is served each course of the meal.

The Savoy Court, leading to the Strand entrance of the *Savoy*, is the first and only road in Britain down which traffic travels on the righthand side.

The Duc D'Orleans, claimant to the French throne, was the first guest for whom the *Savoy* obligingly stamped the fleur-de-lis crest on the crockery and linen he used.

The first "water party" in 1905 was also the hotel's most elaborate, known as the famous Gondola Dinner. Host George Kessler, a Wall Street financier, entertained his guests in a recreated Venice. The courtyard was made watertight and flooded to a depth of four feet, scenery erected around the walls, gondolas built, costumes designed and guests dined in Gondolas on the Grand Canal. Caruso was there as a singing gondolier.

A member of the Strauss family was the first artist hired by the *Savoy* to provide music while the guests dined. The idea, said Ritz, was to "cover the silence which hangs like a pall over an English dining table."

The *Savoy* was the site of the first verbal altercation between Lord Queensbury and Oscar Wilde.

On 29th May, 1913 tradition was overturned when two diners at the *Savoy* got up to dance to the string orchestra. As others followed suit, a space was cleared between the tables and social tradition was overturned.

Dining to music was not new; however, dining and dancing had always been entirely separate activities. Over the next four decades, the *Savoy* became established for dinner and dancing.

Peach Melba was originally dreamed up by Escoffier to finish a dinner celebrating Dame Nellie Melba's performance as Elsa in *Lohengrin*. Melba Toast was also named in honour of Dame Nellie, although in this case, devised by Madame Ritz with Escoffier.

The Pilgrim's Society of Great Britain was formed at the Savoy in 1902 on the eve of King Edward's coronation by Sir William Goode and his American friends, George Wilson and Lindsay Russell. They decided to form a club "composed of Americans like ourselves, who have made the pilgrimage over here and have received and appreciated British hospitality and there will be English members who have made the pilgrimage and discovered that we are not all Red Indians." Soon after, a sister society, The Pilgrims of the United States, was formed.

One of the most distinguished dishwashers to have graced the Savoy's kitchens was Guccio Gucci. As a young Italian in London at the turn of the century, he was so impressed with the glamour and wealth of the guests that he returned to Florence and started his renowned luxury leather goods company.

Omelette Arnold Bennett, named after novelist Arnold Bennett, who immortalised the inner sanctum of the *Savoy* management in his novel, *The Imperial Palace*, was actually invented by the author himself and is still served in the *Savoy Grill* today.

Austrian opera singer Richard Tauber signed his first contract to sing in England on the back of a *Savoy* restaurant menu.

Marconi made the first wireless broadcast to the United States from the *Savoy*.

The two *Savoy* bands, *Bert Ralton and his Havana Band* and the *Savoy Orpheans*, were the first to broadcast regularly from any hotel.

George Gershwin gave "Rhapsody in Blue" its first English premiere at the *Savoy*.

Silent-screen heart-throb George Galli disappeared mysteriously after checking out of the Savoy and was found 35 years later, having joined a Belgian Monastery.

"Charleston Blues," a new dance in foxtrot tempo was publicly demonstrated for the first time in England by Mr and Mrs. Victor Silvester in the ballroom.

The first rider in the *Savoy* ballroom was silent film star Tom Mix and his famous horse, Steed who made a surprise appearance at a banquet in their honour.

The first fireproof eiderdown was provided for actor Lionel Barrymore, who had a habit of reading in bed while he chain-smoked.

The Russian prima ballerina Anna Pavolva first danced in cabaret at the *Savoy*.

Rudolf Valentino's first public appearances at the *Savoy* was when he danced at the tea dansant afternoons.

During the Second World War, when a bomb which fell on the Strand and knocked down the leader of the *Savoy's* Dance Band, Noel Coward stepped to the piano and soothed spirits by singing his own compositions.

The hotel was hit twice in one night by high explosive bombs believed to be aimed at Waterloo Station. The ARP men would come out and sweep firebombs off the roof. The one that blew out the entire riverside front of the *Savoy* was a landmine. It came down on a parachute and landed in a tree outside. Despite these attacks, the *Savoy* never once closed its doors and learnt after the war that the hotel was one of the ten top targets for the Luftwaffe.

Film star Elizabeth Taylor spent her honeymoon with first husband Nicky Hilton in a suite at the *Savoy*.

Sir Laurence Olivier and Vivien Leigh first laid eyes on each other at the *Savoy*.

In a gesture unheard of in Royal Family Archives, the Queen Mother stood to applaud Maria Callas when she arrived at the *Savoy* after a triumphant opening in *Tosca*.

The first wild animal to be brought to a party at the *Savoy* was Billy Butlin's pet leopard who came for a cocktail party to celebrate *Smart's Circus*.

The *Savoy* hosted the first night party for Rogers and Hammerstein's *South Pacific*.

The *Savoy* hosted the launch ball for the epic film *Cleopatra*, starring Elizabeth Taylor and Richard Burton.

The first restaurant guests to order porridge and pea sandwiches were John, Paul, George and Ringo, aka The Beatles, when they came to call on Bob Dyan in 1965.

*Ready Steady Go* hostess, Cathy McGowan, was asked to leave the *Savoy* when she turned up in a trouser suit. In 1967 actress Geraldine Chaplin was also refused admission to dine when she turned up in a suit by Pierre Cardin. A trouser-clad Twiggy retired to the ladies room to change into a miniskirt and was allowed to stay. By 1969, this rule was relaxed.

Bob Dylan stayed at the *Savoy* and was refused entrance to the restaurants as he never wore a tie.

The day after 15-year-old musical comedy star, Tommy Steele left school, his mother took him to the *Savoy,* hoping he would get a job as a pageboy. Tommy took one look at the white gloves and decided to sail to New York the next day. He was later to have his wedding reception at the *Savoy.*

The first celebrity flood at the *Savoy* happened when Elton John let his bath overflow.

During the Second World War, American war correspondents spent a lot of time at the *Savoy*. Titch's Bar became their unofficial headquarters and they remained steadfast clients of the hotel, even after 50 rooms were damaged by a bomb. A Government minister was heard complaining that England's shortage of whisky could be directly attributed to the habits of these foreign journalists.

When the Second World War's blackout ended in 1945, the *Savoy* was the first public building to switch on its lights.

A letter from Czechoslovakia addressed to "The Manager of the Greatest Hotel in London" was forwarded by the Post Office with the note – try the *Savoy Hotel* WC2.

In 1953, HM Queen Elizabeth's Coronation Ball was held at the *Savoy*.

Approximately 3,000 private luncheons, dinners and receptions are held at the *Savoy* during an average year.

The *Savoy* operates its own private electricity generating system, Strand Power Co., supporting all lifts and services in an emergency.

The *Savoy* was the first hotel to establish a hotel management-training scheme. "Trained at the *Savoy*" has become a byword for quality in the industry. Many of the students were given experience for a year before returning to home duties. Others were given the opportunity to attend courses at technical college.

Eight china patterns are used at the *Savoy* with Wedgwood for room service. Royal Doulton in the restaurant, Worcester in the Gilbert and Sullivan Room. Currently there are 230,000 pieces of china and glass in use with a nine-month supply reserve stock. All are made exclusively to the *Savoy's* own design.

# Chapter Three

# HOTEL DU CAP-EDEN-ROC
# ANTIBES, FRANCE

THE SCOTT FITZGERALDS AND SARAH and Gerald Murphy first discovered this hotel in the 1920s so it is partly because of them that this now magnificent hotel is world famous. The history of the hotel is fascinating, encompassing European royalty and millionaires, but in the 1920s the hotel was not as popular, and only opened during the winter months.

The story of Sarah and Gerald going to live in the south of France is very well-known. They had been introduced to the area by Gerald's old school mate, Cole Porter. Their villa, called Villa America, became the meeting place for writers, artists, dancers from the United States and England who went on to become world famous, if they weren't already. Picasso was a neighbor and he became part of the group who partied and swam each day at the little beach nearby, drinking champagne and believing in the philosophy of "Living well is the best revenge." The Murphys became synonymous with glamour, sophistication and wealth.

The hotel used to close for the summer months but one year the Murphys needed extra accommodation for house guests, so the story goes, and they asked the manager to keep part of the hotel open for one summer. Since then, the hotel has remained open and the summer months are now "high season," with international celebrities arriving every day. The top stars and directors who attend the Cannes Film Festival stay there, as it is a short drive to Cannes. Perhaps this is why the hotel rates are so high; until recently they did not take credit cards. The grounds are spectacular and the front promenade down to the Beach Club called Eden Roc, where the swimming pool and exclusive suites and cabanas are found, is one of the most magnificent vistas in Europe. The view from the top step of the terrace was described by Dirk Bogarde as being breathtaking, and anyone who did not find it so, was not worthy of breathing.

The Restaurant faces the sea and the swimming pool which is carved from the rock. It is "the" place to have lunch, and the patio is a delightful, flower filled space with a cool sea breeze on hot days, drifting across the bay. At night the elegant lighting makes the large dining space a fairyland of majestic proportions. There is a separate driveway and entrance to the restaurant aside from the main hotel entrance. The menus are most creative and the Head Chef will come by your table to personally see that you are enjoying your dinner. The scent of the eucalyptus gum trees, the fragrant umbrella pine trees, the unmistakable sound of the sea, the aromas from the kitchen and the view are unforgettable

Scott Fitzgerald began his novel *Tender is the Night* based at this hotel. His characters were very similar to the friends he had at that time. Dorothy Parker stayed with the Murphys and became a very close friend, helping them when things started to go wrong in their lives, when tragedy intervened. The early history of the hotel is still available but as time moves on, those days seem almost irrelevant to the hotel as it is now. Queen Victoria, who loved traveling to the Riviera, Winston Churchill, and the Windsors all stayed there, so the British really discovered it before the Americans arrived.

The hotel is situated on a cliff right on the water overlooking the bay with the Esterel mountains in the background. The gardens are beautifully kept; almost hidden behind the vegetable garden is a small pet's cemetery for the former owner's pets, a charming corner tucked away at the side of the hotel. The red clay tennis courts attract players, most of whom still play in tennis whites, perhaps out of respect for the hotel's reputation of class and distinction. No sweaty grey sweat suits here.

Scott Fitzgerald's opening paragraph of *Tender is the Night* describes the setting and the hotel.

"On the pleasant shore of the French Riviera, about halfway between Marseille and the Italian border, stands a large, proud, rose-colored hotel. Deferential palms cool its flushed façade, and before it stretches a short dazzling beach.Lately it has become a summer resort of notable and fashionable people; a decade ago it was almost deserted after its English clientele went north in April. Now, many bungalows cluster near it, but when this story begins only the cupolas of a dozen old villas rotted like water lilies among the massed pines between Gausse's Hotel des Etrangers and Cannes, five miles away. (Gausse's hotel being the *Hotel du Cap*.")

Graham Greene lived nearby in the town of Antibes and was a frequent visitor. He loved the area when the summer was over and all the visitors had left. He wrote a huge amount of his work when he lived there in a very small apartment. He wrote the short story *May We Borrow Your Husband*, about a newlywed couple, probably staying at this hotel and later on he immortalised the *Restaurant Chez Felix* in Antibes in one of his books.

Greene set much of his writing in Antibes. This is the opening paragraph of a book called *Chagrin in Three Parts*.

"It was February in Antibes. Gusts of rain blew along the ramparts, and the emaciated statues on the terrace of the *Chateau Grimaldi* dripped with wet, and there was a sound absent during the flat blue days of summer: the continual rustle below the ramparts of the small surf. All along the Cote the summer restaurants were closed, but lights shone in Felix au Port and one Peugot of the latest model stood in the parking rank. The bare masts of the abandoned yachts stuck up like tooth-picks and the last plane in the winter-service dropped, in a flicker of green, red and yellow lights, like Christmas-tree baubles, towards the airport of Nice. This was the Antibes I always enjoyed; and I was disappointed to find I was not alone in the restaurant as I was most nights of the week."

Dirk Bogarde acted in the film version of *May We Borrow Your Husband*, which included a romantic lunch scene with Charlotte Attenborough at *Chez Felix*. James Thurber was another writer who lived and worked there and he wrote to a friend: "Nobody could do justice to this blue, purple, warm, snowy melange of sea, mountains and valleys. God, what a place to drive a car in! You're always either a mile high, looking down at the sea, or on a valley floor looking up at a town a mile above you."

Cap D'Antibes and the *Hotel Eden Roc* must be one of the most romantic places in the world.

*Chapter Four*

---

# HOTEL CARLTON
# CANNES AND THE COTE D'AZUR

THE *CARLTON* IS NOW RENOWNED as the centrepoint for the celebrated Cannes Film Festival, when each year in May since 1945, it is taken over by the officials running the Festival, and each country seems to have their own suites there.

However, this hotel was famous long before the film festival started. The history and the architecture has been well recorded. Situated in the middle of the Croisette, the views from the hotel of the Mediterranean are magnificent. A former Lord Chancellor of England, Lord Brougham, is credited with having "invented" Cannes when he was detained there while on a trip to Italy in 1834, because a quarantine order prevented him from crossing the River Var into Nice. Lord Brougham, so liked the place that he built himself an Italianate villa on a hill just outside the town and persuaded those friends who would listen to live there too, especially during the winters, as the climate was so mild. Others also built themselves palatial homes, and the village became a town and prospered.

The *Carlton Hotel* and the *Hotel du Cap at Eden Roc* must be the two most celebrated hotels on the French Riviera. These hotels are situated in the best locations on the Cote d'Azur. The *Carlton* on the Croisette in Cannes, the wide boulevard running along the beachfront, and the *Hotel du Cap* on the tip of Cap D'Antibes. The glamorous *Hotel Carlton*. This is where the stars stay, hold press conferences and give lavish parties. During the rest of the year, business returns to normal and some of the joys of the Riviera shine through without the celebrities and [1]the glitz.

In 1955 Grace Kelly was staying at the *Carlton* for the film festival after making the movie *To Catch a Thief* when she first met Prince Rainier III. They fell in love and were married the following year in Monaco.

The hotel was built in 1911 and it is said that the architect designed the two domes on either sides of the front of the hotel after the shape of the breasts of a famous courtesan of the times, Caroline Otero. She promoted the hotel and ended up being named La Belle Otero.

Auguste Escoffier was employed as the Master Chef and his fame rapidly spread.

The *Carlton's* history has to include the Russians. Russia's Grand Duke Michael helped finance the building. He loved Cannes and promoted the city as "Cannes, city of Elegant Sports." He fell in love with a woman called Sophie de Merenberg and like, the Duke of Windsor, he gave up his throne for a woman, preferring Sophie's love; rather than return to Russia, he stayed in Cannes. This saved his life when the Bolcheviks started the Revolution. The Russian aristocracy came and the resulting Russian colony in Cannes spent huge amounts of money and helped with the building of many luxury hotels.

During the First World War the hotel became a field hospital. In 1922 the *Carlton* hosted the Cannes Conference, a meeting of the League of Nations, a forerunner of the U.N. This meeting was to discuss the Treaty of Versailles. The British Prime Minister, Lloyd George and the Prime Minister of France also discussed the staggering costs of war reparations. During the Second World War the hotel was occupied by the Germans.

In April 2011, the prestigious hotel was sold by the investment bank Morgan Stanley to the Lebanese businessman Toufic Aboukhater, who owns several other InterContinental hotels.

The *Carlton* has been the target of several high-profile jewelry heists. Millions were stolen in jewelry and precious stones. In 1994, and again in 2013, thieves broke into the jewelry store, stealing over $60 million in the first robbery and $137 million in the second. So far no thieves have been caught.

My novel, *On the Riviera,* takes place not while the Festival is on but does begin on the terrace of the *Carlton Hotel.* The protagonist, a mature British actress, based loosely on someone like Dame Judi Dench, decides to retire from show business, become a writer, and live in Cannes.

She has been to Cannes during the Festival before but always wanted to return when it was quieter. She discovers the smaller restaurants in the little side streets behind the Croisette, down in the old port and the town square. The menus include regional produce and after dining on gourmet food at the *Carlton, Chez Felix* and the terrace at the *Hotel du Cap,* which overlooks the famous swimming pool where Cary Grant and Grace Kelly probably swam before lunch, she discovers Cannes' local fruit and vegetable market. Here is an extract from *On the Riviera.* Although it describes the market in Cannes, these kind of markets are found in almost every town along the Riviera: the one in Antibes is even larger.

"The old market is one of the most colorful places in the town. The fish gleaming in the sun, arrive at dawn, the striped awnings covering the various sea food from the morning heat. Nowhere else have I seen such a variety of shell food, fuzzy balls of various colors and sizes, weird looking fish, oysters, and creatures from the sea that I have never seen before. Huge arrays of flowers, sweet smelling roses, dahlias, daisies, deep purple lilac, bunches of mimosa, tulips and bulbs of every color, lilies, peonies and rows and rows of green plants, and flowering shrubs. The pungent smell of the vegetables and fruit, was delightful. Piles of oranges, lemons, grapefruit, melons, apples, grapes and practically any kind of berry you could want. The lively atmosphere was filled with the cries of the vendors and there was vitality in that morning air, which was infectious. The aroma of fresh roasted coffee and freshly baked croissants coming from the cafes nearby, was irresistible, so we would always stop at one of them for breakfast, watching the scene unfold in front of us. The smell of the flowers was overpowering and it was a time when you realized how ancient the tradition of an open-air market actually is, almost timeless. We would walk back with our canvas trolley heavy with produce, looking forward to sampling what we had bought.

The whole town is full of color. The palm trees, the canvas awnings, the shop windows, whether it be the high-priced fashion or the boutiques, the furniture and antique shops, the windows of the art galleries, the hotel gardens or the Croisette itself, it is hard to image an English equivalent."

My actress meets many new people, and I hope the book is an enjoyable read. If you go to Cannes, don't forget to eat at one of the restaurants on the beach. On a sunny day, with the Mediterranean at your feet, it is unforgettable.

*Chapter Five*

---

# CHATEAU CLEWS
# A FAIRYTALE CASTLE

ABOUT TEN MILES OUTSIDE CANNES, in the south of France, there is a fairytale castle called "'Once Upon a Time." Those are the words you will find in stone over the front door.

One dazzling sunny Sunday afternoon I decided to take a local bus from Cannes, and ride along the Riviera as far as the bus terminus. I got off in La Napoule then proceeded to walk down to the beach. I was walking down the road and suddenly passed an imposing archway, I looked through it only to see a long driveway, with trees on either side, and a castle at the end of it. There was a little desk with a girl seated behind it just inside the archway, so I walked in. She was bilingual, so I had no problem finding out all about the place. There was no one else there. The other bus passengers who were tourists I supposed, because they spoke English on the bus, had walked passed it, going to the beach.

The Chateau was closed, I was told, but the gardens were open and there was a documentary film playing in a little room in the Gatehouse, if I would like to view it. So I ended up having a rather special afternoon, all to myself. The film told the history of the chateau and I subsequently remembered that it had been described in several biographies, written about the American Jazz age set who were living and partying on the Cote D'Azur in the 1920s.

Since then I have spoken to many people who know all about the place, one chap actually having rented it for an international conference some time earlier.

It has such a romantic history: about this wonderful couple who bought it in 1918 then renovated it and made it their home. There they had spectacular parties, costume balls, and all the American expats were invited. They were very wealthy, so money was no object. To write about the events they held there would take a book in itself.

I had been living in Cannes for around six months and until then had never heard of it. It is not in many tourist books: that is its charm because there are not many tourists about. I always love visiting a place that is not crowded; this time there was no one else there. The gardens and the walkways were mine alone. Afternoon tea is usually served on the terrace overlooking the sea, but because the *Chateau* itself was closed that day, there was no service there either.

The *Chateau* was built in the 14th Century by the Countess of Villeneuse but over the centuries it fell into disrepair. Henry and Marie Cews bought it in 1880 and Marie lived there till her death in 1959.

During the Second World War the Germans captured it and she stayed on as a maid so she could keep an eye on things. It must have been horrendous for her, but she wanted to stay. All her husband's work was still there.

To begin their story, Henry had been with his father in New York, working as a stockbroker quite successfully, when he announced he wanted to be a sculptor and artist and leave the business. His family was shocked and his father outraged by his decision. Henry was very depressed so he decided to go to Paris and continue with his art regardless. While living in Paris he married a French girl but the marriage didn't work out and he returned to New York and lived with his parents.

Shortly after this he met Louise at a grand party, and decided to rename her, giving her the name Marie, which she kept for the rest of her life.

Several months later they left to live in Paris. He had been working as a sculptor there and they moved into his rather crowded studio on the Left Bank. They were blissfully happy. Marie gave birth to a son, Peter, but the First World War had begun and conditions were very bad, with food shortages and bombing raids each night. Peter caught the Spanish Flu as a toddler, and the doctors advised them to move to a warmer climate immediately. Fortunately the war was over by then.

They moved to the *Hotel du Cap* in Antibes for a month before they found the Chateau. It was an inspiration to them, to renovate, to recapture the uniqueness of the place, to work and to socialize.

After the war, and for years afterwards, they gave lavish costume balls, entertained kings and queens, and became the part of the colorful Jazz Age set. They are mentioned in many biographies of celebrities of that era. Henry continued his work and many of his sculptures can still be seen there.

The story of how they restored the Chateau, then the huge popularity they had, the wonderful work they were creating artistically became well known. Peter, their son, nicknamed Mancha, was part of their dream, their "impossible dream," and his children were responsible for making the documentary which is shown there.

Henry died in 1937 but Marie stayed on till her death in 1959. They are buried side by side in the old stone tower on the property. Before she died she managed to set up a Foundation and a Center for Sculptors and Artists, which is recognized by the French Government as an official American Institute. Artists may apply to stay and study there and learn about the incredible work of Henry Clews.

*Chapter Six*

## VILLA CIMBRONE
## RAVELLO

RAVELLO IS HIGH UP ON the Amalfi Coast and most tourists who visit there seem to want to search out where Gore Vidal used to live. The ancient town hasn't really changed since medieval days. Vidal's villa is adjacent to what is now one of the most exclusive and historic hotels in Europe, the *Villa Cimbrone*. It dates back to the 11th Century but has been extensively renovated in the last two hundred years.

Ernest William Beckett, a British politician, who later became Lord Grimthorpe, bought the villa in 1904, remodeled it and replanted the extensive gardens. There is a fantastic terrace overlooking the cliffs, looking down to the Mediterranean Sea, with statues along the balustrade, built on top of a parapet wall, called the Belvedere, that is truly spectacular.

Gore Vidal wrote: "Twenty five years ago I was asked by an American magazine what was the most beautiful place that I had ever seen in all my travels and I said the view from the Belvedere, (also known as the Terrazzo dell'Infinito) of the Villa Cimbrone on a bright winter's day when the sky and the sea were each so vividly blue that it was not possible to tell one from the other."

Michael Holroyd, the British writer, biographer and husband of novelist, Margaret Drabble, has written a book called *A Book of Secrets*.

*Illegitimate Daughters and Absent Fathers*, which includes the history of the *Villa Cimbrone* and many of the legendary people who went there before it became a luxury hotel. He stayed there several times, and followed in the footsteps of the Bloomsbury Group and other celebrated British writers who discovered this romantic and historic place. Not only is the building very beautiful, but the gardens are now open to the general public. Michael writes: "High above the Gulf of Salerno, some fifty miles south of Naples, is the medieval town of Ravello. Higher still and at the end of two meandering roads from Ravello, you find yourself in a place of fantasy that seems to float in the sky: A miraculous palazzo, now called the *Villa Cimbrone*, which answers the need for make-believe in all our lives."

D.H.Lawrence, walking through these gardens in 1927, wrote that he thought the Villa itself was "a bit too much of a good thing...It feels earthquaky," he told his friend. He was working on his novel, *Lady Chatterley's Lover* while he was there.

E.M. Forster in the autumn of 1901, at the age of twenty two, set out for a year of travel through Italy. In May 1902 he arrived in Ravello, and stayed at the *Hotel Palumbo*. It was there that Forster wrote his famous short story, *The Story of a Panic*. In his collected stories he writes in the Introduction: "I sat down in a valley, a few miles above the town, and suddenly the first chapter of the story rushed into my mind as if it had waited for me there. I received it as entity and wrote it out as soon as I returned to the hotel. But it seemed unfinished and a few days later I added some more until it was three times as long."

Lytton Strachey wanted to rejuvenate the Bloomsbury Group in Ravello. He wrote that he felt as if he was in heaven, or as near to it as you could reach on earth. Many famous visitors came to to stay when Beckett owned it, including Virginia Woolf, E.M.Forster, John Maynard Keyes, D.H. Lawrence, Vita Sackville-West, Violet Trefusis and Harold Nicholson. Beckett had a long friendship with Lord Randolf Churchill. In his biography of Lord Randolf Churchill, his son, Winston Churchill describes Beckett as an intimate friend of his father who stood by him, worked with him and rendered many political services in the years that followed his resignation.

The Villa is mentioned in the memoirs of many of the Bloomsbury Set Group. When Beckett died in 1917 his ashes were brought back to the

Villa and buried under the statue of the Temple of Bacchus in the garden. I read the inscription which is still there a quotation of Catullas.

"Oh what is more blest than when the mind
Cares dispelled, puts down its burden
And we returned, tired from our travelling, to our home
To rest on the bed we have longed for?"

Lord Grimthorpe, and later his favourite daughter Lucille, also wanted to leave a permanent trace of their love for this small town. They were generous benefactors to the local people too: they had strong ties to the town and its inhabitants, who devoted their time to agriculture and raising livestock, the only ways to make a living. They financed road, aqueduct and school building projects, promoted vaccinations and medical assistance and helped the most needy families for decades. They did such good work that they were made honorary citizens. They also left the first, extremely important mark in the consciences of the people of Ravello: real wealth can be found in the conservation and respect for history and the strong, longstanding pride for being privileged in having a prestigious past.

The whole atmosphere in the garden is almost spiritual, and the Villa itself can be seen for miles jutting out on the cliff.

After Beckett died his children inherited the Villa. His daughter lived on there and she became famous as a gardener who bred roses. The Rose of Ravello is attributed to her.

Today, you can just visit the gardens at the Villa if your budget doesn't stretch to staying a few nights there.

My husband at the Beau Rivage Hotel, Lausanne, Switzerland

The Carlton Hotel, Cannes

The Carlton Hotel, Cannes

Villa on Lake Como, Italy

Steam ship on Lake Leman at Vevey, Switzerland

Hotel du Cap, Antibes, France

View from Hotel du Cap, Antibes, France

Villa Cimbrone, Ravello, Italy

Front door of Chateau Clews, La Napoule, France

Statue by Henry Clews

Front courtyard, Chateau Clews, La Napoule, France

My father giving gift to Entally

Cover of one of my father's books

Three generations, with my mother and my son Colman

Group at Theatre Museum

My son Colman in the Champs de Mars in Paris

Ken Starrett on the QM2

At the Algonquin Hotel after The Private Life of GBS

The last night of Cabaret in the Oak Room at the Algonquin Hotel

With Steve Ross at the Lincoln Center. NYC

With my husband Gerald on the QE2

The Colony Hotel, Palm Beach

The Library at the Society of the Four Arts

With Tammy Grimes at the Lincoln Center

Author lecturing onboard Cunard's Queen Mary 2

# *Part Two*

---

## A.A. Gill Started It All

# *Preface*

WHEN I STARTED WRITING *A Theatrical Feast of London*, it was to describe the restaurants and writings of British theatre people, where they wined and dined, as well as the writers who wrote about these places. Graham Greene's favorite London restaurant was *Rules* in Covent Garden, for example, Noel Coward's was *The Ivy*, Ian Fleming's, *Simpsons on the Strand*. These are all still in business and fortunately still retain their unique ambiance. (As my London book was going to print, I discovered a bookful of these actor's favourite recipes: Terence Rattigan, John Gielgud, Rex Harrison and more, so I included them.)

Those writers often mentioned these places in their books, but not often did they write about the actual food! It is obvious they enjoyed the atmosphere and history of the places. In Paris there is a weekly brochure which lists interesting visits and "Conferences," as they are called, organized by guides who take a group to various restaurants, when these places are not busy, and tell you about the history, the chefs and the cuisine.

*A Theatrical Feast of Paris* and *A Theatrical Feast of New York* followed because the subject fascinated me: great actors, writers, artists in their favourite haunts, eating their favourite food. As a student I was so broke, dining in these places was a dream; then later, working in New York and Toronto, I didn't really have that much opportunity, so it wasn't until I started writing these books, interviewing the chefs, researching the histories, that I realized that dream.

51

This book is a part memoir of what came before writing these books, beginning in Tasmania, well before any chefs had discovered the place; then the experience of trying to become a concert pianist, then living in Toronto in the snow, working in The Bahamas in the winter and mainly searching for an interesting life.

New York introduced me to another world within the world of dining. I found I could combine my love of music with the love of food when I discovered the world of cabaret. Not only can you dine on gourmet food but afterwards you are also entertained by musicians who are usually masters of their art, especially in New York and now, miraculously, in Palm Beach. I think I was the first to open a Cabaret Room since World War II in London, which curiously was in the exact location of one of the top rooms now, Crazy Coqs in the *Regent Palace Hotel,* now no longer a hotel. Introducing Michael Law as a solo act, even though he had had his own Piccadilly Orchestra for many years. Ruth Leon is in charge of the room, and there has been an American invasion by New York performers gaining wonderful reviews there, singing among other songs, the great American songbook.

The crowned Prince of Cabaret in New York, Steve Ross, entered my life, and we worked together on anthologies that combined his wonderful talent at the piano with a narrative of the world of international artists. Cole Porter, Noel Coward, Irving Berlin—all the masters—KT Sullivan, the head of the Mabel Mercer Foundation, tirelessly works to preserve all the best music and the bests artists to perform in a yearly Cabaret Convention in New York.

Now in Palm Beach, as the Food and Entertainment Editor at the *Palm Beach Society Magazine*, I review cabaret artists appearing at the Royal Room in the legendary *Colony Hotel* at the top of Worth Avenue, run by the charismatic Robert Russell. This is the hotel where the Duke and Duchess of Windsor stayed and rumour had it that they didn't pay their bill. So, to confirm that they did, they framed their original cheque, which still hangs in the lobby.

But to go back to the beginning. A traumatic event happened in January, 2016 that suddenly shook my world because it immediately took me back to my childhood: the huge disastrous bush fires taking place, in Tasmania where I was born. I thought of my father, a conservationist and ornithologist, and his constant fight to save the great rain forests of the Island.

But two things happened shortly before this. A.A. Gill, the British writer and restaurant critic, wrote a review in the *London Sunday Times* about the Island and I suddenly discovered that my father's book, *Stones of a Century,* had been re-published after 60 years. How is it that when you are suddenly taken back to your early life, that all the memories surface?

I had loved *Around the World in Eighty Days,* but it took me much longer to get around the world. The following account is not how I didn't get to, or play Carnegie Hall as a concert pianist, but how I found some consolation or rather compensation for it. Who cares? I hear you say. And from Tasmania? Exactly. Well I felt vindicated after reading what A.A. Gill had to say about Hobart.

Standing on deck of an ocean going liner at sea reminds one of the first early explorers. Those brave sailors who gazed out to sea towards the distant horizon, perhaps terrified not knowing if and when they would ever see land again. Day after day the prospect of running out of food and water with no idea where they were heading, and perhaps when at last, they did see land, landing in a hostile environment. The same applies to life What is going to happen? Who is going to help you? The sea is always unpredictable, and so is life. We are at the mercy of circumstance.

# A MEMOIR

## *Leaving Tasmania*

IN IRELAND, MOST WRITERS FELT that they had to leave and go to England. "Was there ever an Irishman who did not get himself turned into an Englishman as fast as he could?" wrote Henry Craik. So, too, I thought about Tasmania - not to turn into an Englishman, but I would try to get there so that a little history and culture might rub off on me.

Ironically, it was the Irish who helped populate Tasmania, as a great deal of them were shipped out as convicts in the 1800s, even for such small crimes as stealing a loaf of bread.

When the lucky ones were released from prison, they were given large tracts of land to cultivate and their ancestor families to live on, sometimes with huge sheep and cattle stations across the land.

The British writer A.A. Gill recently wrote in the *London Sunday Times* that he preferred visiting Hobart rather than visiting Rome! He was either being very sincere or has done a good job fooling all of us with his wit. Suddenly I had a large lump in my throat. It was all so long ago, but I remember the place as if it were yesterday. The lump was the sadness and nostalgia for the place I called home.

I was seized by a sudden desire to write a book about the place, but then I remembered how my other books had all started with shitty first drafts, and many re-writes. I have been reading Anne Lamott's wonderfully funny book *Bird by Bird* about the pain and agony of writing a book, and the shitty first drafts, in which probably only members of my family would be interested, if pushed. But also I wanted to suggest that perhaps if we do up stakes and go to live in another country we might discover a wonderful creative life which we may never have the chance to live if we had stayed at home.

Reading Antonia Fraser's recent book about all the writers that had been interviewed, asking them which books they remembered before the age of ten, or what books were read to them earlier than that, made me realize that I didn't remember reading any books before the age of ten. So I must have been extremely deprived. It made me wonder.

Although most people don't know where it is exactly—the little island below Australia—many famous people have been born there and the celebrated war hero, General Montgomery went to school there. Eileen Joyce, the famous pianist, took London by storm and you can hear her playing Rachmaninoff's Piano Concerto in the background of Noel Coward's film *Brief Encounter*. Other notable Tasmanians included Errol Flynn, the swashbuckling actor who retired to Jamaica, Merle Oberon the actress, and now of course, Princess Mary, married to the heir of the Danish throne.

There is also the prize-winning novelist who won the Man Booker Prize in 2014, Richard Flanagan who still lives in Hobart. His novel *The Narrow Road to the Deep North* is about a Tasmanian prisoner of war who worked on the Burma Road for the Japanese during the last war.

Gill describes the glories of Tasmania, the remoteness, the beauty and of course, the food. The island has always had great natural beauty that many visitors have reported on for the past two centuries. Now, since the arrival of the Internet, the feeling of remoteness must have disappeared.

When I read Gill's article, the lump grew larger. How on earth could anyone understand the charm and loveliness where I grew up, when everyone at that time made fun of the island, except perhaps for my father, who loved the island. He ended up in his last job as the head of the Scenic Preservation Board, similar to the National Trust in England. His name was Michael Sharland.

A keen gardener, Lord Talbot of Malahide commissioned and sponsored the book, *The Endemic Flora of Tasmania*. He was a close friend of my father and they often worked together. I visited Lord Talbot at his castle just outside Dublin when he was back in Ireland.

My father was also an ornithologist and journalist who wrote a weekly column called Nature Notes, under the pen name of Peregrine for Hobart's newspaper *The Mercury*, uninterruptedly for over 60 years, which must be some kind of record. He knew the bird call of every bird on the island, including the Lyrebird, known for being the best mimic of any other bird's call, hands down. His books included *Stones of a Century*, his best seller, which tells of the first old houses built on the island following the tradition of great country houses in England. He refurbished and furnished one of them, which is now a top tourist attraction there, called "Entally." He also led one of the last expeditions to look for the famous now extinct Tasmanian Tiger.

I am tempted to write about my childhood but mine would be the same as all other Tasmanian children, and probably most Australians': trips to the beach, climbing mountains, hikes through the bush, but maybe we did more because Dad was doing research for his books and articles for *Nature Notes*.

But I did have a grandmother who owned an antique shop, which was full of treasures, in the center of Hobart. As a young girl I loved going there after school, discovering new things that had come in, finding little ornaments, or wonderful pieces of furniture. Most came from Europe, so I had my first taste of the elegant china and crystal objects often from Austria. While watching *Downton Abbey* I would see some object, either in the kitchen or upstairs that were very similar to things that were in her shop.

She had a back room where we would have cups of tea and sticky buns, between customers, and talk about the new acquisitions. One glorious day, she was called away for an hour or so, and left me in charge of the shop. I was thrilled. Not many pieces had the prices on them, so when I asked what I should quote, she said "everything is two and six." In those days that meant two pounds and six shillings. This became a classic expression in our family, passed down for years, whenever anything to do with a price came up, one of us would always pipe up with "two and six," even after most of us had forgotten where it came from, except me.

Grandmother went alone to England by ship twice, to buy more antiques, and came back with loads of antiques, including six brass warming pans that hang on a wall. These became very rare later on, because the demand for them was intense. Warming pans were filled with hot coals in the old days, and brushed across cold sheets to warm them on winter nights in old England. We also had horse brasses, the little plaques that you find hanging up around pub fireplaces in England, which also became collectors' items. *Antiques Road Show* would have had a field day. Fortunately I still have some of the originals before they started making fake ones.

My two sets of grandparents were totally different. On Dad's side, they had been professional explorers and surveyors of Tasmania. His great-great grandfather was one of the founders of the Tasmanian Club—I believe his portrait is still up on wall there—so ambition, talent and knowledge ran through the family, originally from an aristocratic family in England.

My paternal grandmother was very strict and easily shockable, from proper table manners—you could be banished from the table—for not using them, to who you worked with and what you did with your time. My maternal grandmother came from a working class town in Yorkshire, and was much more down to earth. After building up some capital from her antique shop, she bought Melrose, a beautiful old house, which is still there, on Hampden Road.

When my parents, who were living in Sydney, decided to move back to Hobart, they moved in with her. The house has 29 rooms and a stable, so there was plenty of room. It is still there, except all the glorious trees have been cut down and the tennis court is now a parking lot. My bedroom is an office.

My father was working on the night shift as a journalist for the *Sydney Morning Herald*, but he wanted a day job. I had recently wandered from home and had fallen down a storm drain while he was sleeping. Mother was out, and it seems it took five hours to find me. Luckily, there had been no storms or I would have been washed out to sea.

Grandmother began to take in boarders to pay off the huge mortgage, then she bought two more large houses in Hobart and rented them out. She had a sixth sense about investing in real estate. She was a pretty woman, and dressed elegantly. Rumor has it that when she arrived in Hobart the man she was engaged to had married someone else, so she married his brother. She opened a second antique shop and became friends with everybody at

Burn's Auction House on Collins Street. They would call her if they had some special shipments so she would have first viewing.

When she was very old, I would sit with her in front of the fire, and she would ask me to open one of her many trunks, then take out a jewelry box or two, full of broaches, rings, necklaces and usually gave me something. It was like being in Aladdin's Cave in her small drawing room. There were trunks of furs, evening dresses, beaded evening bags, all kind of things she had collected. I still have the ermine muff she gave me.

Some nights, in the firelight, we listened to radio serials, her favorite one being the dramatization of Georgette Heyer's *These Old Shades*. My brother, Roger, loved the popular serial *In Search of the Golden Boomerang*! There must be hundreds who remember it.

She taught me a dress sense: when to wear long gloves, how to tell real pearls, what to wear when and to what occasion, something that held me in good stead later in life. The trouble is, both grandmothers did too good a job, and I still have to bite my lip when I am sitting with passengers on a ship or at a social function, when they put their elbows on the dinner table, or drink with two hands on a cup. Oh dear! But the worst one is that most North Americans never put their knife and fork together when they have finished eating. I feel sorry for the waiters, who then have to guess if that person has actually finished eating, especially if there is food still on the plate!

So I was ready to join "society" and between the two of them, I had been trained.

Everyone in the 50s and 60s wanted to leave Tasmania. It was almost like the Grand Tour: you first went to London, then Paris and around Europe, before returning home. Then all the girls married, raised children and the men slowly became domesticated and settled down to a comfortable, if boring life. I don't know if it is still the same.

I couldn't wait to leave. I remember attending a symphony concert one night. Hobart did actually have their own orchestra but they invited guest conductors and guest artists to join them, and I wished I could have a conversation with them—about the composers, the scores, their lives—and I hungered for more knowledge. To go overseas was a dream only achieved by their parents who arranged for their son or daughter to do the tour for year or so.

I still remember with awe when a local violinist, Beryl Kimber, won a scholarship to study in London. The world was at her feet and walking home after her farewell concert I was totally spellbound and amazed by her playing and her future as a world class violinist overseas. She had a brilliant career in London and played at the BBC Proms in her first year.

The thought of all this made me even more anguished and frustrated. In those days it really was true that the grass was greener on the other side of the world. But now with the addition of TV and the Internet you can really live anywhere in the world. However, that dull ache of missed opportunities followed me around for quite some time. The ironic thing was that my father was writing about the Island's glorious natural beauty and the uniqueness of the flora and fauna, when all I wanted was the dirt and soot of London, the theatres, the architecture and all that London had to offer.

Why is it that Australians are still considered friendly but a little backward? The accent! Like a friendly hillbilly from Arkansas, they were usually adorned with a broad-brimmed floppy hat, with corks hanging down from it to scare off the flies. It would be interesting to see if people would regard them differently if they were to speak with a BBC accent. I have experimented with changing my accent many times, to fool people, and I discovered a tremendous reaction, from Brits, especially, when they think you are may be an aristocrat from Westminster. Their whole manner changed when they found out you were Australian! It still applies today.

There is still a feeling of superiority in the UK, whether it be social or business, towards Australians. We are still called "colonials"—even more so than Americans—just because we are a young country and therefore cannot be taken seriously, except by Americans.

Gill's article took me back immediately. Yes, our scallops and oysters are the best in the world; the freshest, too, especially if you buy them off one of the fishing boats in the little old whaling harbor at the end of the day. My mother would send me down with an old white enamel billy, to pick up scallops: one shilling for a billyful. They were on the table in just over an hour. Everyone has a childhood story of these kind of things, but not perhaps one of regret.

The last time I was in Hobart, after burying my Mother, and selling the family house and possessions, I went up to the top of North Hobart which looms over Hobart, looked at the unforgettable view of the town and the harbour, and suddenly had an idea, or epiphany, if you like, of what I was leaving behind. A paradise of sorts, knowing it would be just be a matter of time before this place was discovered and all the plots of land, and houses would rocket up in price, which would then triple when people started getting computers and moved there from the mainland. It was one of those moments that freeze in time and you remember vividly years later.

How do you persuade yourself to leave, especially if you are watching an amazing sunset? I was leaving the next day and I somehow knew it would be a very long time before I came back, if ever.

Most people have stories of family outings or holidays they had in their childhood, but not many readers find them interesting unless they themselves were there. I always smile when I see family shots taken at Lyme Regis or Bexhill on Sea or some place in England where the sand is black or grey or just plain mud, and no sunshine at all. Usually cold and windy; the only people who enjoy it are very young children.

How I wish I could take them to my favorite beach - Seven Mile Beach, a few miles from Hobart, stretching between the deep blue sky and azure sea, with white surf pounding on the sand. Pure white powdery sand for miles, it hurt your eyes to look at it in the blazing sunshine. You were surprised if you found any other person on the beach or in the high sand dunes behind, which we would slide down for hours on end. The Bahamas are a runner-up, so you get the idea.

School days were the most interesting when we had Art and Music. I loved art classes and if someone had told me that I would attend the famous Art Student's League in New York one day, I would not have believed them. My work was mostly landscapes. Like Mount Wellington, the large mountain that stands like a giant protector over Hobart. It was like a person when I was growing up. Many people look out of their windows every morning to look at what "the mountain is doing." It has a blanket of snow, or it has disappeared, in mist, or as on one disastrous morning, it was on fire.

The mountain became part of your life. You never forgot it. There it was, rising up behind the city, reminding us that some things never change. Life, birth, death, mortality, it never changed. The zig zag track, which every school kid had to climb, the Fern Tree Valley, the Silver Falls, were etched in every child's heart. The track between Fern Tree and the Springs was a memorable one. Some parts of the track were made from the trunks of fern trees, so it was soft and springy as you walked, almost as if out of a fairy tale. The ferns made a kind of tunnel of green. I do hope it is still there, and I don't want to know if it isn't. Mostly I remember frosty mornings, bitter cold, walking up Davey St to school, looking at the mountain. The exhilarating fresh air was how I imagined Switzerland must be. Mountain air, crisp, cold and invigorating.

The mountain has so many different faces. On the way to the pinnacle you pass through a kind of desolate area. The trees all bent by the wind—the stony view—but then there are the lush parts farther down, and the sparkling waterfalls.

I guess the most vivid thought I have of school was the cold! I was a basketball player, and we would have matches early on Saturday mornings. Some days it was so cold your fingers were stiff, even in gloves; you would have to soak them in warm water before you could hold the ball. Chilblains were the norm. After all, we were the last stop on the map to the Antarctic!

Sometimes we could hear the husky dogs on the ships in the harbor on their way down south. We used to walk down to the docks to see them. But they were on the ships, tucked away somewhere.

The docks were full of ships from overseas. Some were freighters with the name of their country on the stern. I remember the thrill of seeing a new ship from our top floor windows come around Battery Point. One day the *Queen Elizabeth* appeared and we couldn't believe how huge she was.

This was the original one and it was so exciting to walk down to the pier and watch her berth alongside the other ships. The Hobart harbor is one of the deepest in the world, so large ships could dock alongside the pier. As kids it was about the most exciting thing to do after school, then come home and dream about sailing in one of them one day.

Now that they have cruise ships visiting there, the passengers are taken on shore excursions to Port Arthur, a convict settlement where the buildings are still preserved, or up to the Pinnacle of Mt. Wellington where there is a view on a clear day of almost half the island!

At Melrose out by the stable in the cobbled courtyard, there were three rather large rooms with bathrooms that Grannie rented out. I hated going up there because of two incidents that happened when I was very young.

Mrs. Rainbird and her husband who was a driver of a steam roller—machine that flattened asphalt after it had been laid—lived in the end one. Unfortunately, he was away at work, when his wife started screaming and had an epileptic fit. She fell face down in the open fire, and could not get up. My mother rescued her, but I saw her face and will never forget it.

Then the old man who lived next door, Mr Gray, blew up the gas water tank over the bath one day. We heard a great explosion and he came out with a black face, which terrified us. I hardly ever went out there again except to gather firewood, as our woodshed was across the courtyard from them.

At Christmas we would take punnets of fresh raspberries and cream and sit on the beach after perhaps a barbecue of steaks. Pity Paul Hogan ever did that commercial about "putting another shrimp on the barbie," which lead people to believe we all spoke and lived like that. True, there are some great beer drinkers, but no more than in England, with a pub on every corner. Often driving home, we would pass Mum's favorite field: full of wild daffodils. She used to collect armfuls of them and put them in the back of the car. Even though we took many, the fields were still thick with them.

I remember many picnics, again wonderful views as you eat, the smell of eucalyptus and pine trees, the bird calls, and of course, Dad always had his camera at the ready. We once saw a Lyre bird, a rare sighting, as they are notoriously hard to find in the bush. The bird imitated the small whirring sound of a time setting noise on the camera, then the camera click. This was also filmed by David Attenborough in one of his brilliant Bird Series on BBC television years later.

There were also the fishing trips, usually on a very small boat. Then someone would clean the fish, a fire would be lit on the beach at sunset, followed by another memorable meal which I still can taste. The warmth of the fire, after the sun goes down, and the conversations were unique in that Dad would always have some fact or story about the place where we were. The fishing was only part of it.

So A.A. Gill is correct in describing all this, as well as adding the news about the great new Museum, MONA, the Museum of Old and New Art, built by local David Walsh, that has finally brought Hobart some recognition.

Here are two extracts from my father's books. From *Oddity and Elegance:*

True, this island which has been likened to a pendant hanging from the necklace of continental Australia, is by no means an Eden with a pleasant garden about it. Nor is it a paradise where the sun casts its favors perpetually. There is much land yet to settle and mountains to tame. The south-western region is as primitive as ever it was, and the western country little better. The eastern half has yet to be filled. There are still gaps waiting for towns and industries.

But it is just this contrast- the elementary wildness of mountain and gully, the unbridged rivers and tangled scrubs, alongside the homely pattern of farms and old estates, stately parish churches and quaint little villages- that makes Tasmania what it is – a land of oddity and elegance. There is a distinctive flavor about it that carries the hallmark of Tasmania exclusively.

From *Stones of a Century:*

There is no ignominy in living in a State which is much like a museum of history and architecture. There is evidence in fact that those outside rather envy us because of this. They say we are more "history minded" than the people in other States and exhibit a special interest in our historic relics, which is probably true, because Tasmania has a warm, and personal kind of history- one that is associated closely with our own families whose roots go well back down the years. More than a century has passed and we have not forgotten the names of the designers and builders of many pleasing fabrics that grace the land nor the people who first lived in them, for the reason that these were often intimately related to us.

Fine and spacious old houses, although economically unworkable owing to the completely changed labor situation. Some have been converted into flats and guest houses, institutions and hostels: Others are occupied by shepherds or stockmen quite unable to stay the decay and deterioration that goes on around them, so the houses crack and crumble, the outbuildings are undermined by vagrant water and fall in heavy winds, and soon there is a ruin where once noble house stood.

My father would have been very pleased to know that our old ancestral home, Woodbridge, has now been restored and is has been awarded for being one of The Small Leading Hotels of the World!

There is even a Sharland suite, and the new owners have invited me to stay.

My mother worked all through the war for the Red Cross. She organized knitting groups, who knitted socks and singlets for the troops on machines; she distributed books for the wounded men in hospital in Hobart and after I had left Tasmania, she took a job as Supervisor for the whole State of the Northern Territory, from Alice Springs to Darwin. She and Dad would drive the only road between those two outback towns, usually with no other cars or trucks for days. The stories she had of visiting the sick in those outback farms and arriving in Darwin hot and tired. There were no cell phones back then; they were on their own, if the car broke down.

When I was twelve years old, our piano teacher took a group of us from school, to see the film *Song To Remember* which is about the life story of the composer Chopin. Jose Iturbi played the music, Cornel Wilde played Chopin and Merle Oberon played George Sand. I can truly say that film changed my life.

It affected me so much that it propelled me to learn most of the music played in the film, to practice eight hours a day for years, to dream of falling in love with Chopin. In fact I used to pray he would come and visit me in my room: that's how mentally deranged you can get after eight hours at the piano practicing his Polonaise. My music teacher was delighted. I was determined to play that piece at the end of the year school concert in the Hobart Town Hall. I wonder how many people are inspired by one single film when they are young? I was totally changed and I couldn't wait to get to Europe and find out more about his affair with Aurore Dudevant, who called herself George Sand.

I read all the biographies about him, studied his music, practiced, and practiced again. It took months to master the Polonaise and my brother nearly went crazy listening to the piano. My grandmother had shipped home one of her auction finds, a concert grand piano, that came from Paris. Subsequently it travelled around the world. First to me in Canada, then to London.

After seeing the film I was overjoyed when I went home to discover our piano was a Pleyel, the piano that Chopin preferred. In the film there are scenes that take place in Pleyel's music shop in Paris, and the wonderful classic scene when Chopin is seen asking Pleyel to arrange a debut concert for him. Instead, Pleyel dismisses Chopin as an unknown and untalented, when Franz Liszt starts playing the A Flat Polonaise in the next room. Chopin hears him and goes to join him; sitting together, they play back to back, playing two pianos side by side, and Liszt suddenly realizes he is playing Chopin's music and the rest is history, as they say.

The movie is dated now with a rather corny script, but the actual story of his life is true so it is still worth seeking it out. The sets, costumes and music are beautifully done. It awakened in me the determination to work, seek out everything to do with his music, and has continued to inspire me for the rest of my life.

A fellow Australian, part Polish, Alan Kogosowski, has to be one of the world's top Chopinists, but because he would never agree to have an agent, he now gives master classes in Melbourne after a glittering career, for a time, overseas. Do go to the website www.kogosowski.com. He wrote and finished Chopin's unfinished Third Piano Concerto, adding the third movement, playing the debut performance with the Detroit Symphony Orchestra.

When Dad drove me to the airport he thought I would be returning in 12 months, but I had other ideas. We walked up to the plane—no security of course—and said goodbye at the plane's flight steps. I caught a glimpse of the wild daffodils in a field, as we circled around before climbing into the sky. Hello Melbourne, where I was about to board the S.S. Oronsay to sail to England. I won a piano scholarship and unbeknownst to me, my parents had arranged for me to study at the Guildhall School in London for one year.

Unfortunately, just as my father was retiring years later, a real tragedy happened in Tasmania when a group of entrepreneurs suddenly began buying up land and forests, only to destroy them and start logging the timber and completely stripping landscapes of topsoil and the wonderful flora and fauna of the beautiful fern valleys and trees unique to Tasmania. It is still going on and world heritage sites once again have been threatened and legislation changed to allow even more land and forests to be cleared.

Some trees are centuries old, and the bird life is precious. This is a huge conservation issue and one that is tremendously urgent. Naturalists and ornithologists are up in arms and fighting the government all the way up to the present Prime Minister. If only something could be done before all the nature reserves are gone. My father spent his whole life writing about the incredible beauty of the Island, which is about to become a money spinner for developers.

Very recently this tragedy has begun again the destruction of primeval rainforest that has been evolving for millennia or from wet eucalypt forests, some of which contain the mighty Eucalyptus regnans. These aptly-named kings of trees are the tallest hardwood trees and flowering plants on Earth; some are more than 20 metres in girth and 90 metres tall. The forests are being destroyed in Tasmania, in spite of widespread community opposition and increasing international concern.

Clear felling, as the name suggests, first involves the complete felling of a forest with chainsaws. Then the whole area is torched, the firing started by helicopters dropping incendiary devices made of jellied petroleum, commonly known as napalm. The resulting fire is of such ferocity it produces mushroom clouds visible from considerable distances. In consequence, every autumn, the island's otherwise most beautiful season, china-blue skies are frequently nicotine-scummed, an inescapable reminder that clear felling means the total destruction of ancient and unique forests. At its worst, the smoke from these burn-offs has led to the closure of schools, highways and tourist destinations.

I heard that in the Styx Valley, in the south-west, the world's last great unprotected stands of old-growth Eucalyptus regnans are being reduced to piles of smoldering ash. Over 85% of Tasmania's old-growth regnans forests are gone, and it is estimated that fewer than 13,000 hectares of these extraordinary trees remain in their old-growth form. Almost half of them are to be clearfelled. Most will end up as paper in Japan.

In logging coupes around Tasmania, exotic rainforest trees such as myrtle, sassafras, leatherwood and celery-top pine - extraordinary, exquisite trees, many centuries old, some of which are found nowhere else - are often just left on the ground and burnt.

As I am writing this at the beginning of 2016 there is further breaking news that the government is lifting more barriers to logging and allowing further destruction. Sad news indeed. Since then we heard of the dreadful bush fires of January 2016.

# Ship To England

Through the Red Sea, the Suez Canal, the Med, Gibraltar and Spain.

FORTUNATELY I FOUND A SCHOOLMATE to travel with who lived just down the street from me. We had walked to school together for several years so we knew each other well, which was a help in times to come. WHAT TO TAKE? AFTER WEEKS of anticipation and trying to get clothes together, I took far too many, but as it happened, when I got a job in England in Rep, I had to have all my own wardrobe. You did in those days, so it all became useful. Can you imagine a poor working actor having to supply his own good looking tuxedo, a velvet smoking jacket, a tennis outfit, a business suit, a blazer sometimes with a crest on it, for his roles, just to be considered for a job in a weekly Rep company out in the boondocks? Maybe Weston super Mare or Ipswich? Nowadays, we have thrift shops, but when I worked, charity shops didn't exist. Everyone held on to clothes because they had been rationed for so long during the war; you needed coupons to get clothes. In England at any rate.

When we boarded the ship our parents bought colored paper streamers to hold as the ship moved slowly out of the pier. We never thought about leaving the family, I guess because we both had brothers back home and our parents were busy with their own lives. We were too excited and everything was so different. Like hundreds of other girls we were going back to the Homeland and we wanted to see everything.

We shared an inside cabin, that was tiny compared to the cabins today. There was no air conditioning,.except in the dining room. We had a kind of air blower blowing cool air into our cabin. Going through the Red Sea was tough even though we didn't really suffer. We would put our wrists in a sink of ice water and cool off that way. It was all very luxurious, we thought.

Each night our cabin steward would "draw our bath," meaning he would fill the bath then knock on our door. We had a choice of seawater or fresh water. No one seemed to want showers. In those days people all had baths. Don't ask.

There was a dinner gong which was carried through the ship announcing both lunch and dinner.

We were totally amazed at the menus, never having had a formal dinner in a restaurant before.

However, we quickly found you didn't need to order from every course: it just was too filling.

The meals were the focus of the day, because we quickly discovered there really wasn't much to do as there was no entertainment at all. There was a violinist who played during the formal Afternoon Tea, and there was a three-piece band for dancing after dinner. That was it.

My girlfriend was slightly older than me and a few months later in London she told me she was not a virgin, but had had an affair in Hobart before she left. I was very surprised. But it did explain her behavior on board. I must have been quite a bore to her as I was more interested in finding a piano I could pratice on each day, than finding a man. I was happy to practice several hours a day. They found me a piano in the children's dining room. Imagine all the children on board eating earlier than the adults, so there would be no children in the main dining room. If only they had kept that rule.

I thought of my maternal grandmother sailing from England, from Yorkshire, around 1901. It took six months around Cape Horn. What a journey. That would have been before refrigeration, so there would have been no fresh food probably, or milk, unless they kept cows and chickens on board. I wish she had written a report about the journey. Charles Dickens wrote about his journey across the Atlantic, of course, and it sounded horrific. He was very seasick, and wrote that his cabin was coffin shaped, it was so small. Being so ill, he couldn't wait to get to America. Of course, he had to go back by ship as well.

Our ship had the first kind of stabilizers on board but we were fortunate not to have any rough weather. But it took 22 days, going through the Suez Canal. We were so young nothing bothered us.

I had my piano to practice in readiness for my first interview with my music professor at the Guildhall and Marjorie was happy flirting with any man she could find. I was shocked to come back to the cabin one night and find one of our table stewards on the bed with her. He left quickly and I could have had him fired, but I knew that Marjorie had enticed him back to the cabin.

Our first port of call was Colombo. You could smell the city miles out to sea. When we disembarked for a bus tour, we were dismayed to see the poverty and filth in the streets. The men all chewed a beetle nut, which was bright red, and spat it out after it had dried up so the pavements were all covered in red spots, which looked like blood. We were very upset to see the children deformed and sick in the streets. Someone said that their mothers purposely broke their arms and other limbs to make them grow deformed so they would be able to beg more successfully.

The bus took us up to Mt. Lavinia, a posh hotel outside the city. It resembled some hotel in a Somerset Maugham story and I remember we were cheered up by having their English Afternoon Tea in the gardens.

Back on board we sailed through the Red Sea and the Suez Canal, stopping at Port Said. The mountains looked like cardboard cutouts against the red sky at sunset. Almost like a stage set. After the ship docked in these ports, the native boys were everywhere and shouted up at us, come and buy, Mrs. Simpson, or Mrs. Miniver, names they had been taught to say to all white women from the ship. Or the only names they heard in the news, from England or Australia.

There was a very large department store that stayed open till 10 p.m. when the ships were in port. We were amazed at their merchandise: jewelry, diamonds, cameras, leather goods, and masses of silver etc. We had no money to spend over and above our budget and knew we couldn't go over our luggage weight either. The rest of the voyage went smoothly, with stops in Cairo, Marseille and Gibraltar. It was when I was in Gibraltar that I found such a wonderful array of foreigners I vowed I'd go back there one day.

# *London*

AFTER MOVING INTO A HOSTEL in Bloomsbury it was just a day before my studies started at the Guildhall. First it was a visit to the Drama Department which was in the basement. It is hard to forget how out of place I felt. All the students were British and they spoke with cultured accents. I tried not to speak but I was asked questions and felt very embarrassed by my Australian accent, which everybody in the room picked up. From then on I was determined to get rid of it but it turned out to be far more difficult than I ever imagined. Now, of course, all accents are acceptable even though you are taught to speak in the original received accent—BBC.

Everything was strange to me. The snobbery came through immediately, I sensed that I would never be taken seriously until I lost my down under accent. It is a serious thing, but to the British, Australians are still regarded as country cousins as soon as they open their mouths, particularly in the halls of the Guildhall. It was better in the music department because your tuition was usually a private lesson with your piano professor, and my prof was more interested in my playing than my speaking.

After I began lessons at the Guildhall, it was very difficult to find the time to practice the piano, let alone learn new works which was a requirement because of the necessity of increasing your repertoire.

As newly-arrived students, we felt the excitement of being in London. We needed to see all the things we had read about back home. During the first few months, we tried to go to as many concerts as our budgets would allow, and also to see all the great actors who were playing in the theatres at that time. All the legendary ones, John Gielgud, Ralph Richardson, Vivien Leigh, Laurence Olivier and on and on. It was the golden age of the West End.

We were invited to a Garden Party at Buckingham Palace arranged I believe by Tasmania House; we stood at our first Prom concert at the Albert Hall, went to Museums, every weekend catching up on our list. I tried to explain to my professors that I would work harder later in the year, but that it was our first time in London. He said it was up to me, and whatever I thought was important. Of course, it was all important.

The Guildhall posted notices on the Bulletin Board for cheap student prices for most theatres, but then one day there was a notice that any Commonwealth student, (me) who would like to appear at the Coliseum in front of the Queen for a Gala Show which included Australians and New Zealanders, they should apply as soon as possible. Of course I did. Later that month, I stood onstage at the Coliseum singing in a tableau looking up at the Queen and Prince Philip in the Royal Box.

During those first few months, the wonderful part of it was, we never noticed the weather, it rained all the time, but we didn't notice except if we had forgotten our raincoats. I managed to get a part time job as an usher at Robert Atkins's Regent Park Open air theatre. I would dash from the Guildhall to be there for an evening performance, then get back to the hostel before curfew time. Thank goodness I was never locked out. but some of the girls were.

That first year was full of events. I still have my diary from those days and we seemed to do all this for hardly any money at all. But I kept trying to supplement my budget. After the Regent Park Theatre closed for the season, I applied to the St. Martin's School of Arts, and managed to find another part time job, as a model for a class of portrait painters. I wasn't so desperate as to apply for the life classes, because I knew that meant taking your clothes off, and it was much too freezing in London to do that.

There were many Australians living in London in those days. I suppose there still are, but I met none at the Guildhall or at the hostel. I wrote home twice a week. I am sorry that my letters went astray after my parents died, as they covered over 40 years from the time I left home.

My music professor gave me lots of encouragement. I was a little more advanced than the other students, having worked professionally in Hobart giving recitals on ABC radio months before I left home. His name was Dennis Dance and I wondered years later if he was related to the young actor Charles Dance who was making a name for himself on the West End stage. My lessons were twice a week, but there was no piano back at the hostel and I didn't have the money to buy one, so I would go down to the school very early to search for a practice room, which were only free if you got there early enough. It made me concentrate like mad when I found a practice room, because I knew that a Prof would soon show up to use the room for lessons. When my own prof discovered I had no piano, he was appalled and said it was like drawing blood from a stone! No piano!

At the end of my course, he said I was ready to make my debut. Debut? Evidently you hired the Wigmore Hall or some such place and invited journalists and agents to give you hopefully glowing reviews to start you on your way in to the professional world.

Oh dear!I knew my parents wouldn't have that kind of money; also I was having grave doubts about my talent, finally realizing that I did not have that extra genius that makes a true concert pianist who then tours the world and dazzles thousands. Besides, there are dozens of us!

A short time later, because I had taken a drama course, I was a surprised to be cast in the end of term play, which I seemed to enjoy more. Namely, because there was no grueling hour after hour practice at the keyboard.

Before leaving home, I had been given a letter of introduction to Eileen Joyce, the then famous Australian concert pianist I met backstage a few weeks later, after a concert. I handed it to her. I'd been keeping it till I had the opportunity to meet her in person. The next day she phoned me and invited me for tea later that week.

Walking to her studio I felt very nervous, as I was in awe of her. She was alone in her elegant studio. I looked at her concert grand piano and was grateful that she didn't ask me to play. We talked for about an hour, and she told me that even though she was celebrated, famous, successful, she still practiced every day and that like a ballet dancer, you had to be always on form. Practice was the only way to achieve this. She advised me to seek other artistic work. Anything but the piano, I can remember her saying.

Afterwards I walked down her street in Chelsea in a daze, suddenly realizing that I wouldn't be fulfilling my dream of becoming a famous concert pianist, also knowing that I had wasted a lot of time. All those years of dedicated practicing hour after hour, now just all down the drain. It was a shock.

My inspiration from Song to Remember had all been a total waste of time. I knew that this was a turning point and I wondered how I could suddenly change. As it happened, it hadn't been a waste of time after all, because it brought much happiness later on.

# THE OLD VIC

On my walk to the Guildhall School from the hostel in Southampton Row, down the Kingsway, then around Bush House in the Aldwych, I often would drop in to Australia House to read the Australian newspapers, which were usually several weeks old. I noticed a small paragraph that said that the Australian ballet dancer, Robert Helpmann who had been Margot Fonteyn's partner at Covent Garden for so many years, had retired from dancing and had become an actor. He with his partner, theatrical producer Michael Benthall who was a director at the Old Vic Theatre, had organized a tour of Australia with Robert in the lead in three Shakespearean plays together with the actress Katherine Hepburn for six months. I re-read the article. My heart beat faster.! There was nothing I would rather do!

I couldn't believe that this news hadn't hit London yet. That night I phoned Eileen Joyce, thanked her profusely for the tea, and told her that I had found another calling. I was very rude and asked her if she knew Robert Helpmann, and would she call him and tell him about me, an actress and pianist about to change careers. I marvel now at my impertinence but I was desperate; she would either do it or not.

However, I did manage to get an audition with 200 other hopefuls lined up outside the Old Vic shortly afterwards. But I am getting ahead of myself.

My scholarship from Australia was just about depleted but I was determined to stay in London rather than return to Hobart. The funds were supposed to last me one year and with the money my parents had given me, I managed to save nearly half of it, to make it last for another year. Only students who had little money knew how to do this. At the school cafeteria, rather than spend money for a cup of tea, you would have hot water with sugar and lemon in it for no charge and get the soup crackers to eat for lunch. Hard bread buns filling in for later in the day. They only cost threepence.

A fellow student knew a friend of hers who was an usherette at the Old Vic but she was leaving, so they suggested I go and apply. I was interviewed by a dragon lady who said I would have to show up for every show she scheduled. She gave me the job. I would suggest anyone going into the theatre to get a job, front of house, somewhere. That is where you actually meet the producer and the director, in the back of the stalls, on an opening night.

Thus began a memorable six months working at the Old Vic. It was the season when Richard Burton was playing most of the lead roles. Claire Bloom, John Neville, darling Michael Hordern, Fay Compton were all in the company. Every day I would be watching and learning from these great actors. I must have watched Burton play Hamlet over 50 times and I still remember every stage move, including his dramatic duel with Robert Hardy who played Laertes. After Robert nicks his poison sword on Hamlet's bare elbow, during one of their pauses in the fight, Burton slowly turned towards him, realizing what had been done to him, poisoned, and is about to die. The air was magic, you could hear a pin drop in the audience. A long pause with eye contact between the both of them, until Burton rages and suddenly springs on his opponent with his sword in a deadly attack. Soon enough everyone onstage is dead and the audience is electrified by the actor's passion, which no one there could forget in a lifetime. The entrance of Horatio, (John Neville) seems almost an anti-climax, after the bloodbath that took place immediately before. Burton also played Coriolanus that year, Sir Toby Belch, and Caliban in The Tempest. Claire Boom played Ophelia to his Hamlet, Miranda in The Tempest, and Viola in Twelfth Night.

Michael Horden's Malvolio was also unforgettable; it is such a tragedy it was never filmed. He was such a born actor and never had any formal training.

Between the matinee and evening performances, the front of house staff were allowed to eat in the little cafeteria which was backstage, providing simple dishes for the actors who preferred not to go out during the break.

Here I met most of the cast and witnessed some of the funniest dialogue you can imagine between actors who were wired up after playing the matinee and ready for the evening show.

Burton seldom came down but he could be found across the road in the local pub, usually with Claire.

Often he would have had one drink too many, and we would know by watching from out front when this happened. Although this story is sometimes attributed to Olivier, it may have come from Burton.

One evening, he heard a woman seated in the front row loudly whisper to her companion..."He's drunk!"

Burton hearing this remark onstage, turned to the woman and said "Madame, if you think I'm drunk, wait till you see the Duke of Buckingham!"

Another incident occurred when Winston Churchill came to see the play and Burton heard mumbling coming from the front row; he looked down and saw it was Churchill. He was reciting the words along with him. He came backstage afterwards to see Richard, but asked to use his loo before he greeted him.

We were all invited to the Christmas party that year which took place up in the top rehearsal room on a Sunday night. Everyone was there, plus the spouses of these stars. Suddenly there was dancing and a Jolly Miller was announced. In the States I think it's called a Paul Jones. All the woman walk round in a circle clockwise, and all the men anti clockwise, until the music stops. Then whoever is facing you is your partner for the next dance. I saw Burton join the circle. Help! How can I get the music to stop at the right time? I watched carefully, most of the women were not concentrating as I was, there was lots of laughter and joke-telling as the circle went around and around.

Then it happened: the music stopped, and who was opposite me? Richard Burton of course. We danced a waltz I remember, and I told him how I watched all his performances from out front. He was much shorter than he looked onstage, but I was in heaven and then the dance was suddenly over and we went back to the circle. I suppose it isn't such a big thing, but I did catch the magic personality that Elizabeth Taylor obviously caught. People forget how witty he was, and his wit was as quick as someone like Noel Coward's. Funny, erudite, knowledgeable, bubbling up with a smile but also with the sense that he didn't suffer fools gladly. His voice was incredible, deep, resonant, full of feeling, unforgettable. I was delighted to be in the preview audience when he, Rachel Roberts, Emlyn Williams, gave a reading of Dylan Thomas's "Under Milkwood" before it was presented to the public. All Welsh, they captured the atmosphere of the play's setting exactly. Later on they made a recording of it, but we were the ones who heard it first.

To dance with him I was totally over the moon. I suppose it's like dancing with David Bowie, or Sting, or some rock star today, but Burton was such a huge star in those days, with just cause, even though it may sound pathetic these days. I guess like me reading about someone who danced with Henry Irving, or Ellen Terry. Bully for them. Every generation has their idols.

I used to look forward to the matinee days when we could go backstage and eat at the cafeteria. There was always so much fun. Claire Bloom used to bring her little dog and I wondered how she managed to go onstage leaving him in the dressing room, but we never heard him bark. I wanted to be in the company so much it hurt, but at least I was eating with them.

One day, one of the actors was telling about this strange little statue he had bought in an antique shop and everyone pretended to be so curious and fascinated by his purchase he said: "Wait a second and I'll go and get it." He had about four long flights of stairs to get to his dressing room. When he had gone, someone suggested that we all hide. When he came back with his purchase, no one was there: the room was deserted. He asked the waitress who was trying not to laugh, where everybody had gone; he was totally bewildered. We all appeared laughing after he had gone back upstairs. He never forgave us.

I kept waiting to hear when any auditions were going to be held. Dozens of theatrical agents in London were waiting too. Every actor wanted to get into the Old Vic Company. At last a postcard arrived instructing me to report to the stage door at a certain date and time. When I arrived I was devastated to see about 100 actors standing in line at the back of the stage behind the safety curtain. I hadn't expected to see so many and they kept coming. Thin ones, fat ones, tall or short, I didn't recognize anyone. We were all extremely nervous. It was agony waiting for your name to be called. We knew the casting director and several other executive producers were sitting in the dark in the stalls.

I was lucky. When I walked onstage for my audition, they recognized me and greeted me with: "Oh it's you!" I had stood beside them often at the back of the dress circle, when they were pacing up and down on a first night. After I had done my audition pieces, they said: "Where have you been?"

(I had taken a job several months earlier at the Felixtowe Rep.) The next question was rather obvious, I thought: "Why do you want to join the Old Vic?" I think I laughed at that one, as it was so obvious.

It was then that I thought of Eileen Joyce and later asked her if she could help.

Something must have worked, because shortly afterwards I received a letter of employment to tour Australia with the company. It was an unforgettable day. To receive the offer and letter from the Old Vic in a crummy backstage dressing room on a freezing cold morning before rehearsal was one of those moments one never forgets.

# OLD VIC TOUR

The excitement of actually getting ready for the tour was unforgettable. I couldn't wait to go.

To fill in the time I asked two student friends if they would hitchhike with me through Europe to Naples where the ship I was to take had a stop on the way to Sydney. We would start in Norway then work ourselves down to Italy, staying at Youth Hostels on the way. These days, of course, that would be too dangerous, but back then, if you had a Union Jack or an Australian flag sewn on the back of your backpack, most lorry drivers would stop to give you a ride. But three of us was quite a challenge! One of the students dropped out on the third day as it was too rigorous for her.

We started at Newcastle then took the ferry across to Bergen in Norway. The sea was very rough so we stayed on deck most of the night, as it seemed calmer there than in the tiny cabin. Next morning, we walked around the pretty town of Bergen, then later we found the cable car which went up to the Youth Hostel on the mountain behind the city. We were terribly impressed at how clean the hostel was: everything very tidy. The breakfast was fabulous. It was the first time we had seen cheese and meat and yoghurt on the table.

In those days everyone who checked into youth hostels were required to help with the chores. Either in the evening, when everyone had checked in, or in the morning before you left. Sometimes it was peeling a bucketful of potatoes, washing dishes or sweeping out the common room. I have no idea if this still applies today. People were respectful of the house rules, and lights out was strictly enforced, although I don't remember at what hour. You took your own sleeping bag or sheet shaped as a bag and slept on bunk beds. Amazing what you can do when you are so young. I only remember one heavy snorer; the rest were all exhausted, especially the hikers who slept like logs.

On we went through Denmark, Belgium, France and then Italy. I kept a logbook which I still have somewhere, and we always managed to find a hostel, although sometimes they were way out of a city and hard to reach. Most of our drivers drove us there; in return, we had to keep them amused with our stories while they practiced their English with us. Thank goodness we had no bad experiences, which is amazing as we were changing drivers about three times a day. They were mostly truck drivers who were bored and wanted company.

In Naples I got up early and went outside—the hostel was on top of a hill about five miles from the city center—to see if my ship had arrived. I couldn't see it in the harbor so I was slightly panic stricken. Later we caught a bus to the harbor and there it was!! My girlfriends had arranged to go back to London by train but they came to see me off. In those days visitors were allowed on board and they came to see my cabin which was a weird shape: sort of an indoor cabin but with a hallway of about 10 feet leading down to a porthole!! So at least I could see outside. The ship suddenly reminded me of the ship that had brought me to London two years earlier. I never dreamed I would be sailing home to join the Old Vic company in Sydney. Most of the company had gone out earlier by plane.

The sunset that night renewed my romance with the sea and I thought of Homer's description of "the unharvestable sea" but it seemed more Wagnerian to me. The sky was so dramatic, the scene needed music. That romance still exists for me, with the thrill of boarding a great ocean liner. The Maitre'D seated me at the Senior Doctor's table for dinner, and I quickly learned that he was responsible for providing and choosing the wine.

Up till now as a student, I had never been able to step into a London pub for a drink; couldn't afford to and never thought of it, so this was a whole new experience. I knew a little about wine, but not having had any for two years I only remembered the white wines of Australia.

I was rather bored until I met the Irish Junior Doctor. He kept me entertained from then on, whenever he wasn't working. Maybe it was just his impressive uniform. There were no programs organized on board except for a trio for dancing and for afternoon tea. Also, I think, perhaps a movie or two. We stopped at Port Said, Colombo, Perth, Adelaide, Melbourne then Sydney. It was magical.

Once in Sydney I joined up with the company and we rehearsed until opening night. For the opening night, Mother came from Hobart, the only city which had not been included in the tour.

We went from Sydney to Melbourne, then Brisbane, Adelaide and Perth.

During the first week the company had two dress rehearsals and everyone got to know each other.

The leads had rehearsed in London so the all company members were now together.

I only spoke to Katharine Hepburn briefly as she always stayed in her dressing room until her cue. Robert Helpmann was more friendly and did barre work off stage while waiting for his entrance. I was surprised he still kept doing his ballet exercises: probably a habit of years and years. It was second nature to him. I was totally in awe as I had seen him dance at Covent Garden and there I was standing right next to him in the wings. He was quite short but wiry and supple. He had a quick wit and also didn't suffer fools gladly.

At each city on our tour, we were welcomed by the Mayor with a reception and the media. Then a few days later, Katharine would hire a bicycle to find her way around each city and if there was a beach near by, which there usually was, she would go there and search for shells. Helpmann would sometimes join her and it was amazing that photographers couldn't find them. Helpmann once said that if he wasn't gay, she would be the kind of woman he would have married. They were very close all through the tour and they usually went out for dinner after the show. Often she would book a long distance call to Hollywood—in those days they had to be booked—to Spencer Tracey as they were obviously still lovers and talked several times a week.

It was a sensational tour. People lined up at the stage door every night. Gillian, my friend in the company and I would be amused when we came through the stage door, and nobody approached us. We got through the crowd with ease. But because we had very small roles in the repertoire we got easily bored and looked forward to the understudy rehearsals when we had much more to do. Gillian was chief understudy for Katharine, so she had to be line perfect, but she never got to go on during the six months we were touring.

We ended up in Perth and then it was decision time for me. My parents wanted me to return home to Hobart but I wanted to return on the ship with the company. By that time, after saving hard, I could afford to pay for my fare and expenses. It was a tough decision but one they knew was best for my future. It was sad to leave but when there was a chance of continuing in the company, it was my only choice. Little did I know that things would turn out quite differently and my acting career would be changed for ever.

Katharine and Robert flew back to London but the rest of the company had been booked to travel back by ship. I stayed with them. Boarding the ship I wondered whether I would meet the Junior Doctor on this voyage as I knew the other doctor had gone back to Ireland.

We had about eight days before our first port of call. I went on a search for a piano, since I wanted to keep practicing all I had learnt at the Guildhall. There was only a piano in the main lounge, so I judged when it would be almost empty so I could practice. I found that during the lunch hour it was usually empty, so I sat down to play.

That day the Junior Doctor happened to walk through the lounge and heard me playing. He walked up to the piano and stood listening to me. It was a Chopin Impromptu. After I finished, he introduced himself, and said that he played the same piece.

I asked him to play it but because he was in uniform it was not appropriate. However, later on, over a glass of wine, I found out that he had won his University's prize for piano, playing Chopin and like me, had seen *Song to Remember* and had been inspired to learn those Chopin pieces. When he was off duty we spent lots of time together talking mostly about music and getting to know each other.

We went ashore at the different ports; he filled me in on their history and language etc. I discovered he was a classic scholar who knew Latin and Greek and could recite poetry in Greek, Latin and French.

He introduced me to a world so far removed from my own. He knew all Homer's work, and could read it and all the Greek mythology, in the original. It was his lifelong passion. I was totally bowled over.

He had gone to a famous school outside Dublin and when we docked in Southampton he took me there. Also to meet his parents, who lived in Merrion Square, one of those lovely Georgian Squares in the city where he grew up.

He then had to return to sea for another trip to Australia but after that he would be leaving the shipping company and had thought about studying for a specialty in America. He proposed marriage, wrote to my father, and then we were engaged.

I spent about three weeks after he sailed trying to get an acting job. The Old Vic had already chosen the next year's company while we were all away, so nobody had a job waiting for them.

I made the rounds of agents, did auditions, read all the ads, but it was hopeless. It was freezing cold, raining and everything seemed hopeless. There is nothing quite like that feeling of hopelessness when you are looking for work, when freezing to death and with no friends. The company had all gone their separate ways, and Gillian had joined her actor boyfriend who was in Rep in Dundee, Scotland. I will never forget how depressing it was.

Gerald had transformed my life. We were in love, and I thought that being married to someone who actually saved lives, contributed to the community in a positive way, treating sick people, making them better, dealing with the basic needs of hundreds of people was so much more important than what I was trying to achieve. He wanted me and taking care of him and helping him seemed so much more important than trying to strut my stuff on the stage. Besides, no one wanted it! Or me. I also realized that all my work at the piano had actually helped me to find a wonderful man.

While he was competing his last round trip to Australia I took a ship to Gibraltar and then one to Tangier. He wrote from every port. I worked there for eight weeks until we met again when the ship called into Gibraltar and I made the ferry trip over from Tangier to meet him. We made plans. He would go to the States first, and I would follow.

# *America*

I SAILED ACROSS ON THE SS France in a six-berth inside cabin! It was very rough and I was seasick for most of the trip. It was totally awful. But then we arrived in New York. Wow! I walked down Broadway looking for a lot of white buildings: that is what I thought the great White Way was! I had my first American milk shake; it was fantastic. Then I left for the airport. I caught the plane to St. Louis where Gerald was studying to become a psychiatrist.

We married a week later and had two guests at the wedding. The whole thing was simple but we wanted it that way. We drove up to Canada for our honeymoon, and saw Chris Plummer playing Hamlet at the Festival Theatre at Stratford, Ontario, a lovely old town, now really totally unrecognizable.

Back in St Louis, everything was so big! The cars, the houses, the meals. Eating out was cheap and we loved the bars and Dixieland bands that played across the Mississippi in East St. Louis. Little things were noticeable. How they had little bags of sugar on restaurant tables: no sugar bowls caked with wet sugar on spoons, as they did in London. Paper napkins in boxes, individual salt and pepper envelopes, rather than half empty pots on the table. I was very impressed with the cleanliness of everything.

One of the most enjoyable times was when we used to go to the Crystal Club where Mike Nichols and Elaine May were first starting with the Second City group, playing every night in a kind of black box theatre. It was the first improvisation I had seen, and they were brilliant.

Later, of course, they took Broadway by storm and the rest is history. In desperation I joined the local Amateur theater Group acting in several of their productions, trying to master an American accent.

Gerald finished his training and qualified as a psychiatrist at the Malcolm Bliss Hospital, but he was not allowed to remain in the US so we had to choose where we wanted to go. One evening a former colleague phoned him from Canada and said there was a job they wanted him for in Toronto. So the die was cast.

When the time came we piled all our possessions in the car and drove up to Canada again. After lots of paperwork and immigration forms to fill in, we arrived in Toronto with great expectations.

Those first months were awful, especially arriving in winter. Nobody warned us! But at least they knew about central heating, thank goodness.

Spring arrived, then summer; I was pregnant so we were house hunting. After feeling very cramped in a sublet small one bedroom apartment, we saw an advertisement for a large country house for rent about 40 miles north of the city, for the same price. It had been totally renovated, with a new kitchen and was newly furnished. It sounded great! That Sunday, a lovely summer day, we went to look at it, fell in love with it, and rented it. Little did we know that it was right in the middle of what they called the snow belt in Ontario. What idiots!! Nobody told us.

A few months later the snow came. The house was a few miles in from the highway on a small side road, and after even a small snowfall, the road was blocked, and not cleared for perhaps 24 hours. Gerald couldn't get to work, and I couldn't have my regular checkups with the doctor. Even before the snow came, I found it very lonely living out there, with nobody to talk to. The nearest farm was a couple of miles away, so I often drove into town as well.

We were forced to move back to the city, and as the landlord would not let us out of the lease, we could only afford a room in a motel, close to the hospital where Gerald worked and where I would go when my time came. It was not good. The house stood empty, we lived beside a chain-smoking cigar lodger who lived in the room next door to ours. The stench was horrible. We had no fridge, so we would put milk and perishables on the window sill, even though it was usually frozen when we needed it.

I auditioned at the CBC for work. In those days they had a very active Drama Department that produced one-hour plays for television every week straight to tape. They were looking for professional theatre actors who were used to that technique, rather than film, where you stop the cameras.

After my son, Colman was born, we stayed in the motel because the snow was still falling in February. It was too icy to take a pram out or even walk because of the slippery pavements.

On weekends, if it was warmer, we would drive up to the house, but then spend most of the time there shoveling snow from the driveway and cleaning up the winter mess.

The CBC dropped their Drama Department, much to the dismay of hundreds of actors who immediately were out of work. Later on I worked for summer stock, and all the same actors were doing that too.

Barry Morse, Gordon Pinsent, who made that wonderful film with Julie Christie, *Away from Her*, Barry Baldaro, Joyce Gordon, Ted Fellows, whose daughter, Megan, became famous playing *Anne of Green Gables*. We toured every week between Port Carling, Huntsville, Lindsay, Peterborough and Coburg, which had a theatre in their old Court House building. Barry Morse went on to make films all over the world, and also was one of the founders of the now famous Shaw Festival at Niagara-on-the-Lake. He also initiated the first Retirement Home for Actors in Canada: PAL. The Performing Arts Lodge in Toronto.

Is was he who inspired me to write another play, *The Private Life of George Bernard Shaw*, because he was an authority on Shaw and had either played or produced every play Shaw had written. He presented the play at the Lodge using all the CBC actors, then later at the Theatre Museum in London at the age of 80, playing Shaw.

One day I persuaded a CBC radio producer to let me interview Canadian filmmakers who were in the south of France, for the Cannes Film Festival. I had read that Canada was well represented that year, but was amused to see subtitles on the films if the actors were speaking French Canadian French. Of course, I wanted to see the great stars as well. Dirk Bogarde was a favorite, and he lived close by Cannes. I had seen all the Doctor films including *Doctor in the House*, then when I met Gerald, who looked rather like him, I was smitten, especially as he was a doctor!

Cannes and its surrounding areas must be one of the most scenic, poetic, and inspirational places in the Mediterranean. But there are dozens of places! All with an atmosphere uniquely their own.

My novel *On the Riviera* tries to capture the feeling of the place, just as the street artists do on their colorful canvases on display along the Croisette.

I went there several times in the next few years, working on different projects. One job was representing Pan Am Airlines at a conference. I loved that airline. On another trip, I managed to find Dirk's house, after much searching, because it was so hidden! He wrote wonderful books, especially *An Orderly Man*. He bought an old olive farm and was blissfully happy there. He wasn't home when I found the place, but his longtime companion took the book I had brought for him to sign and a few days later I received the signed copy with a note from him.

In Toronto, our son was born nine months later but we were still busy trying to find a home. We hadn't enough money to buy a house, so after we gave up our house in Bradford, we rented for several years. I found that there was only one professional theatre in the city and of course, it was deluged by hundreds of out-of-work actors.

I auditioned for the Stratford Festival Company, only to be told that they only hired Canadian actors with Canadian experience. That wasn't true, but what could I do? I quickly became depressed and wondered what I could do; certainly not the theatre.

One day I found a tiny little shop, empty, in an old part of Toronto called Yorkville, where there were a lot of art galleries and very few other shops. I had found a dressmaker who was very talented, quick and cheap, so the idea of opening a little boutique with one-of-a-kind dresses suddenly came to me. I enquired about the rent and it was so reasonable and without a lease that I was very tempted.

Gerald and I were about to pay over a thousand dollars for a one-week trip to Paris to visit Art Galleries, and I thought that after that week, I would be back here, still with nothing to do, so why not put that thousand dollars towards some dress materials, patterns, and rent the place?

It was a good decision. My dressmaker had other dressmaker friends, and I quickly had enough colorful dresses to open a shop. I had a huge Union Jack painted on the front door, and printed carrier bags with the same design. In fact, if you look closely during the opening credits of the TV show *A Time Goes By* with John and Norma Major, you have a glimpse of a girl walking with one on Carnaby Street. It was the height of the mini skirt, Carnaby Street and Mary Quant!

After the shop began to make money I flew to London and bought trunkloads of Quant and other designers. Out came the electric dresses too, ones that shone in the dark. I hired a photographer and some models, and sent the photos to the fashion editors of the two main Toronto newspapers. It was terrific when I got a two-page spread in the *Globe and Mail*, Canada's national newspaper, and when my newly-hired accountant phoned to see how much it had cost, he was amazed to hear that there was no fee: the editor wanted to feature them. The owner of the only other shop that carried Mary Quant also phoned and accused me of hogging the market: she was furious.

Eventually I sold the shop and contents just as the craze for hot pants began—and hot pants for men!

During those years I flew to New York and bought crazy designs from Paraphernalia and Betsy Johnson who is still designing.

My restlessness was rearing its ugly head again. I enjoyed the challenge of starting the business, promoting it, even opening a second shop, but then came the sameness of each day, the long hours sitting in the shop waiting for customers, always a pain. But I did it for six years.

Gerald and I took a week's holiday in Paris. One night as we were sitting by the Seine at sunset, I had this enormous urge to live there, to actually live there as a Parisian! No matter how difficult it would be. Life suddenly seems very short and if you wait to do something, perhaps in in the future, it may never happen. Gerald was working hard in a good job, my son was a school, although not very happy, and I always wanted any child of mine to be fluent in French, because it was so difficult for me to learn the basics. I thought it has to be now!!.

We arrived back in Toronto to deep snow and freezing winter. Where to begin?

# *Paris*

EVER SINCE I HAD ARRIVED in Paris all I knew was that I wanted to stay, to live, to work in that wonderful city. To experience the changing of the seasons, their celebrations on Bastille Day, their customs and food planned for Christmas and other feast days, to discover the charm of little known museums, historic places and above all, the theatre and restaurants. But my French was not good, and I needed practice, so where on earth would I find a job?

My lucky break came one morning while I was walking around the Champ de Mars, "Field of Mars," the vast public stretch of parkland in the 7th arrondissement between the Eiffel Tower to the northwest and the École Militaire (Military School) to the southeast, one of the most charming residential areas in Paris. The area was named after Mars, the Roman god of war, and its initial purpose was to serve as a training ground for military maneuvers. Today, lakes, ornamental ponds, winding walks and grottoes adorn the area, which is home to many birds and one of the rare places in Paris where the song of the tawny owl can be heard at night.

I decided to venture onto a side street, chancing upon a building called the American Library. My curiosity aroused, I found the door open and walked right in. I found it a fascinating place, and after listening to various conversations among the staff at the front desk, I soon learned they were shorthanded, it seemed, so I started talking with them and ended up asking for a job. This seemed to be the perfect place – the timing was right, and I ended up working there for two years. Every day I walked to work from the little hotel we were staying at, and the beauty of the Paris knocked me out. Each morning I would walk across the bridge beside the Louvre, along the quays, and passed the bridges, the open markets, the fabulous buildings, the fruit shops and the cafés.

The job at the Library proved fascinating. I immediately met all the subscribers, all the newcomers at the Front Desk. Most Americans living in Paris came in to borrow books or read magazines and newspapers from the States. If we were not busy I would talk with them, ask why they were here, how long they had been here and found out about their work and lives in France. There was a two-hour lunch break and a half-day off. It was heaven to go back into the stacks and delve among books that made your mouth water. Signed editions of Gertrude Stein and Hemingway, plus all the French writers, many translated into English.

After a few months of this, an idea began to form in my mind as to how I could combine living in Paris, working in the theatre and keep acting as well. There were many French students coming into the Library to read American and English playwrights. They waited, sometimes for weeks, on a request list for the one-act plays of Pinter, Albee, Tennessee Williams and any new plays that had been written. There was no possibility any of these students seeing these plays on stage in English. They had to go home and try to sit and read them with the aid of an English or American dictionary.

I thought: why not present these plays to them in English? These plays were set for their University exams: they had papers to write on them. Wouldn't it be a lot easier for them if they could actually see the play?

There were other reasons too – it would give French students the opportunity of seeing well-known plays in English, it would provide entertainment for English-speaking tourists and residents who didn't know enough French to go to a French play, and also function as a showcase for new plays and performers from the United States and England. It would fulfill a need, as far as the students were concerned and also give new playwrights who were writing in Paris a chance to present their plays too.

Sounded great. Paris. My own theatre. The toast of the Ritz. Discovering new playwrights hidden in garrets in Paris, saving them from suicide. Seriously though, I thought there might be people working in Paris who would be interested. I used to pass Sylvia Beach's old shop every week and remember James Joyce, Samuel Beckett and all the other writers who had a tough time of it in Paris. Maybe there were a few now, in our generation, writing and not hearing from New York for months on end.

Then I met Roland and Jennie. They were there for the same reason that I was, to experience the city, to learn French and to create and express something of themselves in some way – any way – if they could just get it out from being all bottled up inside. They had brought their three-year-old with them from Ohio, so they were more restricted in their activities than I was. Nevertheless they had managed to find a place to live, and the fact that they had both started to write impressed me immensely. Both of them had worked in the theatre back in the States, and they were enthusiastic about my idea of forming a theatre company in Paris. Roland became our first Director.

So now I had found a structured life at last. I found an apartment. I could speak French well enough to get along at dinner parties – the ultimate test I think – and I had found something I really wanted to do and could see more point to doing it than anything else at that time. There is a time and place for everything and this was it, as far as I was concerned.

We started advertising for authors and scripts. From ads placed in the Paris papers we received replies from all over France. It seemed as if there were American writers hidden away all over the country – from the Loire, the Indre, the Basque country down to, or rather up to, Normandy.

Some of the plays were in verse, some were all four-letter words, some were pages of revue skits, some were long one-act monologues from freaky people. We read them all and were amazed that these people had actually found places to live in the French countryside and that they had organized themselves to such a degree, had the tenacity and money to stick it out then sit down and write. It was difficult enough to do it in Paris, but deep in the country somewhere, where the heating probably never worked, where the isolation, the plumbing, the physical discomforts must have been even worse to put up with than in Paris.

Auditions were held, and we chose a company of actresses and actors, some of whom were from the States, others from England and Canada. Rehearsals started on a verse play by a chap from Sussex who was now living in Normandy. He wrote a cooking column for *Vogue"* magazine every so often, so we knew what he did for fulfillment if his writing wasn't going very well.

That was one great advantage of living in France – when things got really rough or really rotten, you could eat. And eat the most heavenly food you can imagine. There was always that perfect piece of Brie and fresh bread, with a carafe of wine or some glorious pastry, or delicious pate, waiting at practically every corner in every village or at your local market.

It seemed to make it all worthwhile. The frustrations, the rages, the confusion of just-where-do-think-you-are-going-with-your-life, can be countered by the complete sensual enjoyment of the country in the spring and summer and sometimes autumn, after a delicate lunch in the country – three or four courses perhaps, tiny courses of perfect food with a good wine. These were the saving graces that could carry one through the toughest of times.

Anyway, to get back to Paris. We started rehearsing the play. The actors were good. We were all working for practically no money but we felt we were doing something worthwhile. The rehearsals were very long, held in cold rehearsal halls – we worked hard and often in places where we were freezing to death.

The French staff at the various rehearsal rooms thought we were stark crazy, and said so. An English-language theatre in Paris? Who would go? We were presenting plays that had never been done before, anywhere, and in English. Perhaps when we did Tennessee Williams or Albee or Pinter, someone might come. Maybe those enthusiastic students from the Sorbonne who could digest anything, but always seemed to have an intense fascination with the American Red Indian, would come. I can't tell you how many French students I met in the Library who would read anything they could get their hands on about the "Peaux Rouges." We met one guy who was leaving his wife, child and a newborn baby to go off to some Mid-Western university to take a course about the Red Indian.

There was no time left to sit around and discuss the policy of the theatre, the use of drama, the "meaning of theatre." We had to get on with it. I met at least two people who had tried running a theatre there before, and they said we were mad and that we would never survive, no one would come, and that if we had any success – financial success, that is – we would be closed down by the French authorities on some cute pretext, such as that we might be putting French actors out of work.

Next, the search for a theatre began. We wanted a small place with an intimate atmosphere. I criss-crossed Paris day after day looking in all kinds of places. Some were absolute gems – an old theatre in a private "hotel" or an ornately carved assembly hall with minstrel gallery still intact. But they were always too big, or too small, or the rent was too high.

It took three weeks before I found "Le Poteau" on the Right Bank. Le Poteau means "the post" and we soon found out why. There was a post just right of centre stage holding up the ceiling. But oddly enough it didn't look too bad.

I knew as soon as I walked in the door that I had found our place.

The theatre itself was tiny with banquettes around the walls and a bar at the back – the "ambience" was terrific. As for the post on stage, well, it just made the stage directions all the more challenging. The actors had to be on their toes if they didn't want to crash into it every so often – and bring the house down in more ways than one.

We moved in with our props, wardrobe and gear and started final rehearsals for the first night, a first night that seemed headed for disaster. The leading lady had caught the flu and had lost her voice, the leading man refused to follow the stage director's directions and had resigned a week before the opening night. He said his contract wasn't binding (it wasn't) – so we were left with their two understudies! For our opening night!

One understudy was a theatre student, not really experienced enough to play a lead, and the other male understudy was a part-time ballet dancer, who was not really suitable for the heavy male lead required in the play.

To say that I didn't sleep very well that week would be a ridiculous understatement. I wanted to phone all my friends and beg them not to come on the opening night. The publicity was already out. Ads in the *Pariscope* and the Paris *What's On* etc. Everything was just too late to stop or to do anything about.

Only one week earlier I had received the theatre posters and was terribly impressed with them. I suppose only someone with an ego as large as mine would appreciate what it is like driving around Paris and sticking up posters of "our theatre" – I posted a lot of them myself for the pure pleasure. It felt great sticking on one at "Le Dome," "Aux Deux Magots," "La Rotonde" – all the cafés where Hemingway and Fitzgerald and the "lost generation" hung out. It didn't matter to me really that I was about 30 years too late to impress them or entice them to my theatre.

It was a mad afternoon going around the Left Bank dropping off these purple posters, then driving home again along the Boulevard St. Germain and seeing them all staring out at me. But that was last week. This week was different.

I felt like disappearing and letting the stage-manager take over till after the first night. But as founder and producer what could I do?

The night before opening night my next-door neighbor, a violinist with the Paris Symphony Orchestra, decided to practice his violin. So with the violin and the tension of opening night, my sleep was racked with more than the usual nightmares most performers go through before an opening night; except I wasn't performing—just sitting in a (perhaps) empty theatre: me, and the drama critic from the *International Herald Tribune*, both of us watching a disaster take place up there on the stage. Why is it that our dreams are often far worse than anything that happens in real life? Terrible nightmares, open graves, that sort of thing, we never experience in real life. Why do our bodies create such awful things that we cannot control?

But as we all know, some of our worst fears never come true. Some, mind you, but not this one.

The opening night was a success, and it was some kind of miracle to see people coming in the door and not turning away. It was a miracle! People kept coming in: we had no place to seat all of them. There was standing room only for our first night! Tom Quinn Curtis from the *Herald Tribune* came and was kind enough to give us a good review and say nice things about us.

We had begun.

Our second production was a crazy comedy by the English playwright N.F. Simpson, *A Resounding Tinkle*. This play is filled with funny non-sequiturs and silly things about unusual people. It was a risk to do it because we didn't know whether our French audience would understand any of it. But we wanted to do it and hoped that at least the French students would catch some of the funny lines. Lines like:

BRO: "Oh hullo, Uncle Ted, where did you park your motorcycle?"

UNCLE TED: "On the spare lot, behind Rachmaninoff's Second Piano Concerto."

It was a bit difficult for an English-born playgoer to follow, let alone a Frenchman.

One evening we had a Frenchman sitting alone in the third row listening intently to everything that was said. He seemed to understand English very well. Suddenly he went into absolute hysterics, doubling over and then falling backwards in his seat. This happened approximately every five minutes or so, especially when any actor made his entrance. I couldn't figure out if he really could understand all the dialogue – as I said, it was pretty funny – or whether he was laughing hysterically at the acting, the costumes or what. I only knew that he was a great lift to the audience and loved by the cast.

We kept seeing new people and talking with writers. Every day I met people who were either screaming with rage over life in Paris, or in fits of depression, or in raptures of delight, or bored out of their minds, or inspired and stimulated beyond their wildest dreams. It happens this way, you can experience all these things within the course of, say, one week. Especially if you are trying to write, or paint or follow some creative endeavor, all the time. The actual "feeling" and nervous energy, if you can call it that, is what Paris is all about, as far as I'm concerned.

The theatre was a great release. We rehearsed, we talked, we sat in cafés after work, in marvellous art deco-cafés with great faces of interesting characters surrounding us – stimulus for playwrights searching for characters – and all of us in the group felt we were achieving something, though we weren't sure what. Admittedly we weren't writing the plays ourselves, but we were in contact with the people who were, and with people who had the same nervous energy we had.

Is it just student "neurosis," this nervous energy to create? Sometimes I think it is, but then, how come we still have middle-aged writers? They must have screaming fits of rage, despair, hope, depression, suffering, just as young people have. I would like to hear from writers who don't suffer any more.

Sometimes after the performance at the theatre I would stay behind in the bar and talk to any patrons who had stayed on to have an after-play drink. I talked to a lot of tourists too – couples from the Mid-West or Canada or the English provinces, people who didn't understand French well enough to go to a French theatre, or didn't want to go to another strip-show or a movie with sub-titles, and so would come to us. I used to talk to the women if they stayed – mostly housewives on a one-week holiday in Paris, or perhaps a school-teacher or nurse who had read our ad. I'd search their faces for signs of what kind of lives they lived; it fascinated me.

Having our own theatre in Paris we were on our way. We were reading scripts from writers living all over Europe. The mail was a delight. That was one of the great pleasures about the whole venture. Now at last, after years of just receiving bills, handouts, local folders, church newsletters, auction sale announcements, more bills, traffic tickets, overdue notices, I was receiving fascinating letters, plays, resumes, life-stories of people I could identify with, ideas, scripts for revues – all of which was more broadening than any cocktail party introductions or dinner party friends, which I had had a steady diet of for years.

There were some days when I felt we were achieving a great deal, and other days when it seemed that we were all just working very hard, being very idealistic and not achieving very much at all.

We still met in cafés after the show and discussed our aims and future plans – hour after hour. I felt the aim of the theatre was to promote new ideas and most of all to promote "thought." I didn't want to present plays which didn't do that. To make people stop and think about our play was what mattered to me most.

But some of those early days were hell. First of all, there were the terrific mood swings of everybody concerned. It is not unusual, I'm sure, in any troupe who are working together, but it seemed harder starting a new venture and a new company, then trying hard to be as idealistic as possible. My own mood swings were very hard to cope with, especially as I was living on my own with no one to discuss the finer details with, the decisions, the overall plans that had to be made. The company was pulling its weight, working hard, but I was the one who had to make the decisions.

The company would change and casts would change too. We couldn't pay our actors very much so they usually had to move on – back to the States or England.

We had a nucleus of about ten people who stayed, however, and most of them had part-time jobs in the daytime, teaching English part-time or working in offices, or studying at the University with a grant from home.

Fortunately all of them had worked professionally in the theatre, so we had a well-trained group who were, in general, as enthusiastic as I was.

The cold weather seemed to keep people away from the theatre. Our theatre, anyway. We worried about insufficient heat in the theatre, and whether people would return if they thought much about how cold they were; we prayed for an early Spring.

The theatre was full of people with colds, coughs, sinus trouble. My God! I was beginning to feel the whole of Paris was full of people with colds, sniffers, coughers, spitters and more and more coughers. One night standing behind the bar, I nearly went out of my mind listening to them and could easily have wrung the necks of everybody sitting in the audience. Shut up! For Christ's sake! Or Get out! I had to get out.

I walked across the street to the corner bistro and ordered a brandy at the zinc counter, where even the barman coughed. When would Spring come? This was getting impossible. We couldn't go on much longer this way. All of us were getting very frayed and most of the troupe had to go home to freezing rooms after walking along freezing streets after being in a freezing theatre all evening.

Needless to say, the theatre owner would do nothing about improving the heat – it was "on" after all, he would say; "What more can I do?" He would say this every week with a typical shrug of the shoulders and out-stretched palms.

We decided to close for a week and those of us who could get out of Paris would go down south for a while to start making plans.

It was on one of my "up" days, or rather "up" evenings, when I arrived at the train station to catch the train to Cannes; otherwise the whole thing would have been a disaster.

I had thought of flying down, but to miss all that glorious French country between the Loire Valley and the south coast seemed sinful. So I thought I'd try seeing some of it just once, then after that one could fly, guiltlessly over it forever after.

You are asked when you buy your ticket if you want to go first or second class, and do you want a couchette? I said "second class" and "yes," I did want a couchette, a small bed, usually bunk type, three each side of the cabin, one of top of the other. Better than sitting up all night, as the train journey took 12 hours, starting at 6 pm.

I found the platform and the train, the guard showed me onto the carriage and then to my compartment. He took me straight to the cubicle with the six couchettes, pointed to the middle one, said "Voila" and then disappeared.

Maybe we all have countries waiting for us which will show us what we really should be doing. What you are doing now might only be a shadow of what you really could be doing in Australia or Spain, or wherever.

I certainly wouldn't have been running a theatre back home, for example. The idea never occurred to me.

Perhaps that is one of the reasons why France means so much to so many people. It provokes so much emotion, either rage or pleasure, that one is constantly seeking expression and release—the stimulus and frustrations of one's own goals—seeing new horizons, new work, and generally growing by having to pull oneself up by the hair roots, or whatever the expression is.

Back in Paris again and back to work, the weather was warm, the company rested. Enthusiasm had returned and once again we felt that what we were doing was still as worthwhile and as fresh as when we first thought of the idea.

We were rehearsing a new play by a playwright from Tennessee and we were sure it would be our best production to date. It was a comedy and the parts were well written. The critic from the *Tribune* thought so too, and we had a good run and good audiences for the play. If this sounds as if things were running smoothly and we were all sitting around congratulating ourselves, then I am giving a false impression. I don't think anything, or anybody in any relationship can run "smoothly" in Paris for more than, say, two days at a time.

It's just something about the city that does it

During these years I followed the theatre in Paris as well as my knowledge of French would allow. In the first year I would take an English or dual script of the play with me to the Comédie-Française. I discovered the seats where the bright overhead safety lights were left on. They were like EXIT signs but without lettering. However there was enough light to be able to read the English script at the same time as watching the play on stage. Also, listening to the play on tape in French at home and following it in English was very helpful.

If other theatres had plays I wanted to see, I would try to read the play first even in French, as then I could at least understand most of the action. Modern plays were more difficult because the language contained more slang and colloquial idioms, like, for instance "I've got other cats to whip."

Often there were interesting lectures on Sunday nights at the Palais Royal which were difficult to follow at times, or dramatizations of the life of Oscar Wilde or Alfred de Musset or George Sand, usually made up of dramatic scenes, with music when appropriate. They were elegant soirées which were cleverly devised and produced. How fascinating it was to sit in one of the most beautiful theatres in France watching French actors recount the life of a celebrated artist or writer.

Some days the fatigue and anxiety of a long week spent coping with the language, the housekeeping, the travelling, would be relieved by going to an American bar and having a few strong gin-and-tonics. It was a curious thing however, that the well-known cocktail bars of the 20s, the Ritz, the Bristol, the Hôtel Continental, were usually deserted at 6 pm. We could never figure it out whether we were too early or too late.

Theatre actors were held in high regard and were more respected than cinema stars. Jean Piat, the French equivalent of perhaps Nigel Patrick, Simon Williams, Alan Alda or Simon Callow, was not only celebrated for his work as a classical actor, but also in Boulevard theatre, popular, modern theatre. Most of his contemporaries worked more in the theatre than in films.

Occasionally, visiting companies provided some English speaking theatre. The Abbey Theatre from Dublin played for a short season in *She Stoops to Conquer* and the National Theatre came as well. The other source of enjoyment was following the up-coming programs at the Olympia. Although music-hall, it had the same excitement as New York's Radio City Music-Hall or the Palladium in London. French stars have all appeared there, including Edith Piaf, Charles Aznavour, Yves Montand, Sacha Distel and visiting stars such as Liza Minelli and Jerry Lewis, who was adored in Paris even though his act included his speaking nonsensical French but with the right gestures. Most Parisians regarded the Olympia as the home of the superstars.

If you enjoyed meeting these kinds of celebrities, all you had to do was to visit the little bar which was just around the corner from the stage door. I discovered it when I went to interview Sacha Distel for a magazine article. But maybe that secret has already been discovered.

Paris was not an easy city to live in. It was more difficult than New York or London. Not only the language but day-to-day routines were so different. In New York there were many stores and cafés open 24 hours, Duane Reade being one of them. But in Paris, if you wanted to go grocery shopping after lunch, forget it. Everything was closed till late afternoon, except the supermarkets which are hell on earth compared to those in the U.S. or the U.K. Transportation was more complicated and tiring, long passageways between subway stations and the air much dirtier than in other cities. People were less polite, especially shopkeepers. I used to think that their bad tempers were because of the cheap red wine they drank at lunch and then tried to sleep off without success.

When the weather turned cold it was far more bitterly cold than anything I'd known elsewhere. The damp iciness was unforgettable; it lingered inside stairwells and passageways that never seemed to get warm, even in summer. It was a particular cold that was extremely depressing, as it came with a cold grey mist and bleak skies. I remember visiting the Lachaise cemetery on such a day; death seemed to be very gruesome and near, with the chilling silent tombs on the other side of my path. Chilled to the bone was an apt expression.

But for whatever misgivings I might have had about the climate, the thrill of being in the middle of one of the greatest cities in Europe, and exploring so much historical and culinary culture more than made up for the physical discomforts. But all good things come to an end. Gerry was far more busy back in Canada, and an offer came that he couldn't refuse. Our son missed his school friends in Toronto and when one of the French boys stole his precious stamp collection one day, he was heartbroken and he also wanted to return. He had visited the famous stamp market in Paris every Saturday and spent his weekly allowance on buying and trading stamps. We returned to Toronto but after they had both settled in, I once again, found that there was no theatre work there so it was off to New York.

# New York

ARRIVING IN NEW YORK, EVERY actor reads the trade paper *Backstage*.
Now of course, it is online, so you can find what auditions and work are
available by searching those pages. I started by going to cattle calls, at
the Actor's Equity office, only 45 steps from Broadway. Producers had to
advertise their casting calls by law, so even if they had already picked their
cast, they would still go through the charade of auditioning. I thought that
was really a farce, but went anyway, because at least you were being seen
by someone. Not necessarily the casting director, as their work had already
been done in most cases.

There is a notice Board in their lounge announcing out-of-town
and touring productions, usually again already cast, and notices for
accommodation, travel discounts etc. Very occasionally they give out free
tickets for Equity shows.

To get an audition, you had to be there very early, as soon as they
opened, to sign up on the list, with no idea, of course, what time you would
be seen. On freezing mornings I would get there early, then have to return
later, maybe around 3:00 pm to be seen. It was extremely depressing. I got
many auditions; it was always the same question: what have you done in
New York and where can we see you?

Like the coach before the horse: how can they see you if you can't get
a job? Even though I had worked with the Old Vic Company in London,
they had to see your work in New York. In those days no one had videos
or demo tapes.

One bone-chilling day, walking home, totally discouraged, I suddenly stopped in my tracks, hit by a small epiphany. It was so obvious. What I was doing was a total waste of time! I decided that I would stop going to auditions, stop beating the pavements. I would sit down and write a play, with a lead role for myself. Then I would get a theatre to produce it and thereby get an agent to come and see me.

I was determined. No more auditions. I was at least going to give it a try because nothing was happening.

I quit my day job as a Receptionist at Elizabeth Arden on Fifth Avenue, behind the famous little Red Door. One of the perks of working there were the free hair do's and makeup.

In the beginning I was delighted to join such a famous and prestigious company but I had been there for several months and was bored out of my mind. There were funny times, however. My job was to make appointments in our third floor Beauty Salon. Most them were made by phone. We had a package called 'The Main Chance Day" that was a day-long makeover of your face, hands and body at around $500. One man called to make an appointment for his wife, which I thought was unusual, and he asked for "The Last Chance Day" which sent us all into hysterics. Did he have a mistress or another wife waiting in the background, we thought? We eagerly awaited her arrival the following week, trying to keep straight faces as we took her coat. She didn't look so bad, we thought. There was another package called "The Visible Difference Day," named after the new cosmetic called Visible Difference. Again, some husband phoned and asked for the 'Physical Difference Day.' Wow! What did he expect, we wondered?

The chief receptionist was a witch. She and her assistant would deliberately let the phones ring and ring before answering them, or they would answer and say "Please hold," then put down the phone on the desk when we were not busy. They wanted to give the impression that our phones were ringing off the hook, when often they weren't. Clients got tired of waiting and hung up, which defeated their purpose, as we lost those bookings.

Some of them would come in every morning to have their hair done then perhaps a massage. It just wasn't my scene. I guess they had nothing else to do. But this was New York after all and they may have been going to balls, opening nights and parties every night. But I had found a new life, I hoped, as a writer.

I forced myself to sit at my dining table and start writing a play. Try it sometime! The realization of the lost income from my job gave me extra motivation. No fooling around. I read books on how to write a play, but after working week after week in weekly Repertory I sort of knew the structure and scene order, but nevertheless it was very difficult. I went to the great Public Library Reading room on 42nd street, a wonderful room, and worked there. The atmosphere gave me inspiration. I had to write a play! Anything that helped: atmosphere, exercise, reading, walking. It all helped.

I read that Noel Coward wrote a play in three days! Unbelievable. All his plays were still being performed around the world and his biography written by Cole Leslie was my reading treat. I read it over and over. Such success, but not till after lots of hard work.

I based the play in Sydney. It was a comedy and I tried to bring in some Australian idioms and jokes.

The lead was a bored housewife, not exactly in the suburbs, but someone hundreds of people could identify with. Someone who, like me, who had an unfulfilled ambition. I never forget those lines in the film *Shirley Valentine,* when Pauline Collins says: "It is all inside me and I can't get it out. What are we supposed to do?"

Finally it was finished. I sent it out, and it came back, many times. I tried to get a play agent; no luck, but I kept at it. In desperation I started pounding the streets, looking up theatres Off Broadway and Off Off Broadway. Every afternoon I would visit one or two. I would ask to see the Manager/ Director but most of them were in rehearsal. I would leave a copy of the play with a covering letter and a stamped addressed return envelope. I had no idea if anyone would bother to read it or even open the envelope. Weeks of this. Some scripts were returned but no letter or just a brief typed form letter: thanks, but no thanks.

One evening I attended a tribute to a great theatre woman in New York, Jean Dalrymple, and onstage she named a young director who she had helped find a building near by which had three theatres in it. She said he would be busy filling the three theatres. Next day, I looked her up in the phone book and found out she lived just a block away. I wrote her a letter asking if I could come and see her. Nothing ventured nothing gained. She was elderly and I thought possibly lonely, even though she had had a lovely tribute.

I received an answer, and to cut to the chase, I met her, told her about my play. She suggested I send it to this young director. It worked, with her name attached. I met him, and he gave me a date, He read the play of course, and wanted to direct it with me doing the casting!

Little did I know how difficult this would be. None of the actors could do a believable Australian accent! It just didn't sound right with American actors. By this time, I was so involved with getting the play on and doing rewrites that I decided I'd rather sit at the back of the theatre as a playwright to see how the play worked, than play the lead. For some reason I felt that the play was more important than just acting in it. Don't ask why. In the end we found a British actress for the part, who could do a passable Australia accent. She had friends in Earl's Court, renamed Kangaroo Court in London.

I wrote a second and third play, all produced at the American Theatre of Actors on the West Side. One day, I received a letter from the Australian Film Board who had read in an Australian newspaper of my search for Australian actors in New York and they were interested in seeing my scripts. Nothing came of this because the chap who wrote to me left his job and no one followed up.

It is customary not to have the playwright in rehearsals, so I spent my time sending out press releases and doing publicity because the theatre did not have the finances to have a press agent. Besides, they had two other theatres running as well. The theatres was usually well-attended and they had an Open Air Shakespeare Festival each summer as well.

When I first came to New York and before I got the job at Elizabeth Arden, I applied for all kinds of work. I left my resume and waited. While trying to write my third play the phone rang; it was from a chap at a well known travel agency who put together various groups. They had interviewed me months earlier because of my work in The Bahamas and said they'd contact me if something came up. Was I interested in taking a group from the San Diego Zoo on a Safari to Kenya for ten days? We would start around Nairobi in jeeps. then fly over to the famous Safari site on the other side of the Riff Mountains. I phoned my long-suffering husband who was working in Toronto and he said whatever I wanted to do was fine, but watch out for the deadly snakes, ho ho.

I had read about the Mathaiga Club in Nairobi; the notorious Happy Valley set, the book *White Mischief* with the unsolved murder of a British aristocrat—recently solved. It all sounded very exotic and romantic. It also gave me a break from playwriting, so I accepted. It was a nightmare. The tour company ceased operating shortly after we arrived in Africa because of the local people's hostility to tourists and the subsequent murders and riots. But that is another story. I found the safari disappointing— the land so dry, dusty, parched, compared to the beauty of Tasmania. We saw all the animals that the group had been searching for, sitting up some nights in lodges till 3:00 am, in the local zoo on our last day there. It was a photo op they had missed during the safari!

It was a relief to get back to the play, and New York.

The only way to get a play on it seemed, was to have a deadline. Actors had to learn their lines, the set had to be finished and the curtain must go up. A few months later we were two nights away from opening night, when the phone rang. I picked up the phone, and it was Dad's doctor from Hobart.

Holding my breath, I waited to hear the news. Oh what timing! Please, please let everything be all right.

My heart pounded. I had been home on a trip within the last year and Dad had seemed well enough.

It seems that he had had a heart attack, that he was in hospital and that it may be necessary for Dad to have a pacemaker. He said it was not urgent but that I should be aware of his condition. Because of this, he was moving both of them into a nursing home near our house, after he was released from hospital.

Anyone whose life has been suddenly interrupted by such family news, knows what the feeling is like.

What do you do? Suddenly the play seemed insignificant. I phoned my brother in England and was relieved to hear that he had already booked a visit and was leaving in a few days. I explained my situation and he said I should stay and come out later, which I did.

Dad lived on for several years and I was thankful that I was home when it happened. I had arrived the day before.

The play was a success. We even managed to get a small review in the *New York Times* written by veteran columnist Edith Nemy! The assistant to the Broadway producer Alexander Cohen, a huge figure in the New York Theatre phoned to reserve. I was over the moon! But the show opened in the middle of the Jewish holidays in September and they were all going out of town.

# *London*

---

I RETURNED TO LONDON AFTER both my parents had died. I wanted to be where we all lived together when they stayed there, to go to the places we enjoyed. Dad, always the naturalist, loved Regent's Park and on weekends we would visit special places outside the city. Gerry took time off from work and joined me there. We rented a flat and I started working again in the theatre. This time, there were no more auditions. I wanted to work for myself. I'd spend hours reading the theatre news, trying to see where I could fit in.

Actors will tell you that they always worry about where their next job is coming from. What a life, even if you have made it and are in a play in the West End. You have to keep in touch with what is going on via the grapevine. You have to be thinking who you should be calling, writing to, emailing all the time. Keeping in touch. You have to be like quicksilver and keep you ear to the ground, so to speak. Who is casting? Is it a film, is it a series, is it for TV? Only an agent who is dealing with all these things knows who's who. Or the age-old saying: you have to be at the right place at the right time.

The tension and the stress will be with you for most of your career. So perhaps this is a lesson that should be taught in every drama school. Getting your first job is hard enough but that was only the beginning.

The fringe theatres were doing some great work, especially the Kings Head Theatre in Islington. Several plays had transferred to London's West End from there and the director, Dan Crawford was building a great reputation for the theatre. We all wished however that he would fix the toilets and the backstage areas, which were disgusting, and maybe still are! How he could ask people like Vanessa Redgrave and Judy Campbell to work there beats me.

The bug was still with me. One day I walked passed the shop called Angel on Shaftesbury Avenue which rents and sells theatrical costumes. In the window were several wonderful costumes and jewelry for characters in various period plays. A world of fantasy, they fascinated me. I wondered who had worn them. or who would wear them. When, where? What if I wrote a play about these costumes displayed there so beautifully in the shop window. It was like finding a trunkful of treasures. Do people still have a clothes trunk for dressing up?

When I got home, I started writing a play about a wardrobe mistress, a frustrated actress who irons and mends costumes of characters and roles, roles she always wanted to play. I took it to Dan at the King's Head. He liked it and put it on. In the end I cast three different actors to play one week each. One of them substituted a couple of monologues from plays she had always wanted to play. Recounting a part she would have liked to play but never did.

Harold Pinter's plays were very popular at the time. I had been to see several of them, and I hated the long pauses, the significant grunts, the whole dramatic structure. So I wrote a short play, "It's Too Late" satirizing this process with a cast of four. It was produced at the King's Head after the *Wardrobe Mistress* and I still keep in touch with the actors who were terrific. We certainly enjoyed performing it. David Bradshawe played the lead.

One day I visited the Theatre Museum in Covent Garden, only to discover the most amazing exhibition of British theatre ever seen in London. There were three long galleries with large windows showing various ages of Theatre history. One window held costumes worn by Laurence Olivier, another window showed Noel Coward's memorabilia, his dressing gown, his music, his various gifts to famous actors; next to it, a window showing Lilian Baylis's desk, her gown, her papers. She was the founder of the Old Vic, then further on, Ellen Terry's gowns, etc. There was the little upright piano from *Salad Days*, donated by Cameron Mackintosh; there were models of the original Globe Theatre and around the corner, I came across a small auditorium.

I was fascinated to know what sacrifices all these legendary actors had to make to pursue their careers.

The anguish of often having to choose between their careers and their private life. For the next week or so I read up about the lives of Henry Irving, Ellen Terry, Sarah Siddons, all the legendary actors through the ages.

Three months later I had a script called *Love From Shakespeare to Coward,* with excerpts from their lives: Poems, poetry and prose about the sacrifices and loves of their lives. But I needed a well-known actor to lead the cast of four. Why not start at the top? Don't ask me how I found the phone number of Corin Redgrave, a member of a fine theatrical family, and Dan Thorndike also a member of a well loved theatrical family, and Sybil Thorndike and Lewis Casson, still remembered for their brilliant careers, but I did. And they agreed to take part for two weeks at the Theatre Museum.

Everything fell into place. The London *Times* published a large photo of the two of them reading together on the first night. Corin spoke about his father Sir Michael Redgrave in the first half of the evening. I was delighted to meet Lady Redgrave, the former actress, Rachel Kempson, after the show. Later on that year, after visiting her for tea, I wrote a play for her and as the Theatre Museum was closed by then, we put it on as a reading at the Club for Acts and Actors. She was in her late 80's and was only strong enough to have one reading, but it was a thrill to have her. Vanessa and Corin came and we all went out for dinner afterwards.

The anthology was published curiously enough by Applause Theater Books in New York, so I found other venues to perform the piece casting young actors so they could do a showcase and invite agents and producers to see their work. London is full of hundreds of them, and I think there should be some kind of regulations for opening a drama school anywhere, because these girls are so gullible, they train and graduate then find that there is no work to be had.

If only the legitimate drama schools could tell them.

My energy was running out, casting and rehearsing a different show every week. I decided that it was time to move on. A few months earlier, someone suggested that I present the show on board one of the cruise ships, as an after-dinner entertainment. I wrote to Cunard and they forwarded my letter on to Diane Coles, who later became a soulmate and close friend until her untimely death. Diane was in charge of the libraries on several ships, as well as setting up a program on board the QE2 for writers. She started a Literary Festival on board. She came to see one of my shows and said it would be perfect for the QE2, so another part of my career started. It is still going on.

Diane was in charge of stocking all the libraries on board the Cunard ships, a huge task. The company is still called Ocean Books. She asked me to be her North American scout for best selling authors. I was flattered by her offer, but rather unsure that I could find these authors. But I was determined to try. By the end of the month I had made a list for her approval and then started contacting the authors through their agents. It was a super job talking with publishers about offering my favorite authors, a free trip across the Atlantic in a First Class suite, everything included, as well as a book launch and signing of their latest book.

I suggested George Plimpton to be the first host. He was such a charismatic man who suggested several other writers such as Tom Wolfe and Gore Vidal. I received a classic note from Vidal saying that he couldn't think of anything worse! If I had offered him a suite on the old Queen Mary, to dine on pheasant under glass, he might have considered it. I framed the letter. Not even a thank you!

Tom Keneally, Bill Bryson, Tina Brown, Harold Evans, Helen Gurley Brown were just some of the authors I invited. Jaqueline Mitchard who had just written a huge best seller called *At the Deep End of the Ocean* was hard to reach. Her book had just been discovered by Oprah Winfrey, so she was in big demand.

After about a year of booking writers, I told Diane I would really like to be able to do a trans Atlantic crossing and she said "Well, write a book!" Wow. It was that straightforward. So after weeks of brain storming day in and day out I thought of a book about my anthology, then decided to write about producing *"From Shakespeare to Coward."* It wasn't so easy. But it also occurred to me that perhaps we could do the anthology on board. So it happened. A few months later, I sailed from New York to the UK.

I presented the anthology with the help of the Cruise Director, Peter Longley, and Alastair Bruce of Crionaich who most recently has been seen as the historian and social advisor to Julian Fellowes on *Downton Abbey*.

Hugo Vickers, the British writer, who writes about royalty, starting with his book on the Duchess of Windsor, was a favorite of mine. He was, and still is I am sure, such an elegant, charming and modest man with deep interest in unusual people. One book, about Baron de Rede, who saved the historic Hotel Lambert on the Ile St Louis, is as fascinating as his other books on royalty.

John Miller, who wrote the four biographies on Dame Judi Dench, also wrote about John Gielgud. He was a delight and we still keep in touch. He organizes wonderful charity events in the UK, booking famous actors to join him. He has written the definitive book on Dame Judi and they often work together on charity events. Also John Bridcut who makes brilliant documentaries. I have written about what it is like to board and sail on a Cunard liner—which of course is far different from a cruise ship—in my first volume of *Classical Destinations*. It is still a thrill to walk up the gangway even after so many sailings. Trouble is that Cunard spoils you for any other cruise line, because the atmosphere is still very British on board, with a British captain and officers, if you are patriotic at all.

Some people say that people born on an island, have a natural love of the sea. I really don't know, but it has been one of the most enjoyable times in my life, sailing on these ships. Certainly because it combines being on stage and performing, traveling, and living out the fantasy of meeting Somerset Maugham-type characters on board. I keep in touch with many of them. Long may Cunard continue to reign, as the most elegant ways to cross the Atlantic.

# The Bahamas

THE BAHAMAS. THERE ARE 700 hundred islands in the sun. Another totally new experience, never to be forgotten. Tasmania has a different kind of beauty; it has the same long white sandy and deserted beaches, but usually not the warmth or tropical atmosphere of the Bahamian Islands.

I had just had a miscarriage at seven months, and it had been a horrible experience in the hospital. Not only the event itself, but how I was treated; so I had to get away from the icy cold.

Gerry took time off and we flew down to Nassau in The Bahamas for seven days. It was a package tour with everything included. These packages were very popular; so much so, that the travel companies running them used to charter several large planes to accommodate all the Canadians who were trying to escape the winter blues. The whole place just knocks you out on your first visit. Warm, humid air, greets you as you step off the plane, and in those days, a calypso band greeted you, playing Island songs, usually with a native girl nearby offering you a local rum punch. A Bahama Mama or Yellow bird, a mixture of several kinds of rum. We were in heaven. The hotel was surrounded by Hibiscus vines and bushes everywhere. The food was delicious, with lots of fresh fish and fruit. I was well and truly hooked.

I felt like Shirley Valentine. (For anyone who doesn't know of her, she was a bored British housewife from Liverpool who escaped to a Greek Island.) We returned on a second trip and a third.

One evening I started talking to the Tour host employed by the Tour company to take care of Excursions and hotel requests, who sat in the hotel lobby most evenings for an hour or two. It seems she was leaving to go back to Toronto and they were looking for a replacement who could speak French. This was for the French Canadian passengers who numbered about a thousand each week. Each host had to give an Orientation speech during a Welcome Rum punch party at each hotel. In English and in French. What a job!

After hearing that family members could fly down on the company's plane at the weekends, free of charge, I discussed the idea of applying for the job with my husband. He had often said how guilty he felt back home, when he was so preoccupied with his work. He loved it, but realized how miserable I was, especially about the freezing cold.

Cutting to the chase again, I got the job and worked there for the next three winters. While there I looked after five hotels in Freeport. My first week on the job was Christmas week, I was so happy but it was a shocker.

Some of the hotels were very short staffed, so there was a high turnover of staff. What happened was really not surprising. There were four planes coming in every Saturday night with around 200 passengers on each plane. Part of my job was meeting these new arrivals, the groups at the airport and putting them with their luggage on buses to the various hotels. As well as saying goodbye to the departing passengers, who were reluctantly returning to Canada and the snow.

Hopefully the hotel staff would be there to meet them and give them their rooms keys.

As I said, this was my first week on the job, and I accompanied the last bus to the final hotel. When we arrived, we found that there was a large Welcome Rum punch party going on for a group I knew nothing about, who had already arrived! But not from Canada, I quickly found out.

The hotel had double-booked the hundred or so rooms, and my group were now on the doorstep to the lobby, tired after their plane journey from Canada. Wow. Quel problem! I kept smiling. Obviously they were all invited to join the party, which gave me enough time to phone around and see where I could find rooms for the late arrivals. It was Christmas Eve. Everywhere was booked! Eventually I found a hotel which wasn't under contract to us, and they took them in.

I finally got to bed around 2:00 a.m. at another of our hotels. Thank goodness the night manager was kind enough not to call me an hour later, when the first call came in from that hotel saying that four passengers had been sent to the local hospital with food poisoning. Worse was to come. Most of the other passengers were ill too. It must have been the conk fritters at the party.

Later that morning, I was surprised to see my Canadian boss and two other officials walk into the hotel, having flown in from Canada. News had spread and they didn't want any of this leaked to Canadian newspapers, of course. Luckily, because of the glorious weather, the passengers seemed to recover fast and the rest of the week went smoothly. It was an initiation I hadn't expected. Most passengers enjoyed their stay, except I felt sorry for the ones, sometimes whole families who had saved up all year for this holiday, if it rained all week they were there. I tried to plan indoor activities and drive people around in the car I was provided with, but stuck in their rooms, they started to complain about the wallpaper and pictures being crooked. I wondered what I had let myself in for. If a group turns nasty on you there is nothing you can do. I had been warned; thank goodness this didn't happen.

Weeks passed so quickly. I loved it. There were many places to take my guests. Each evening we had a different place to go. It was all pure escape. I had lots of free time during the day when everyone was at the beach or playing golf. I noticed there were many yachts in the two boat marinas that were flying Canadian flags, so one morning I walked along the pier and introduced myself to anybody who was up on deck. I had done some radio interviews at the Cannes Film Festival the previous year for the Canadian Broadcasting Corporation. I thought my editor might be interested in interviewing some of these Canadians.

Next day I took my tape recorder with me, and managed to interview two or three yacht owners. Basically theirs were predictable stories. Most of them were living out their retirement dreams. Buying a boat and living in the Bahamas. But sad to say, most moved on after a year or so, mainly out of boredom, lack of activity and/or drinking too much. Many of them, if they stayed, became alcoholics. Others found their families were unhappy, even though they had been thrilled at first. It was an eye opener, and all rather sad. A few kept busy, read a lot, and island hopped over to Eleuthera or Harbour Island, both being fairly close.

The winter came to an end, then our company concentrated instead on sending passengers to Las Vegas or California in the summer, still taking reservations months in advance for a Bahamian Christmas.

It was always a shock to fly back to Toronto. I found it more difficult each year. For some reason there didn't seem to be much happening in that city. During the winter I had met a very talented Bahamian singer, Wendel Stuart, who ran his own night club in Freeport. He was a cross between Sammy Davis Jr and Harry Belafonte. He had the vitality and charisma of Sammy but with Harry's marvellous voice. He sang the Island songs as well as his own compositions. He asked me to help him try and get a job either in Canada or New York, as his night club closed in the summer months. There were no tourists!

One morning I read a small article in a Toronto paper that caught my eye. Two producers were opening an office in Toronto to promote and begin a weekly T.V. Variety Show called *The Palace,* starring the singer Jack Jones, with different celebrity guests each week. A similar format to the *Ed Sullivan Show.*

International celebrity guests such as B.B.King, Cher, Ethel Merman, Lou Rawls, Diana Ross would all make the trip to Toronto to appear with Jack Jones.

Canada was a popular destination for American performers. Pierre Trudeau was the Prime Minister at the time. There were rumors he was dating Barbra Streisand as well as moving in entertainment circles, both in Canada and the States.

Well, this was my chance. I had to get Wendell on that show somehow. He was unknown outside The Bahamas, as he had no agent, but if I could get them to hear him sing, it was worth a try. Here we go again; it was survival time again in Toronto.

Somehow I found out where they were opening an office. I went there, but it was locked. I went again the next day and found someone delivering office furniture. I asked when the occupants would be there. They said the following day. I went there again, there was a painter in the next room, so I sat on a sofa in the waiting room and waited. When the two producers arrived they were surprised to see me waiting in their office. I had determined I would not leave until I had a job.

They knew they wouldn't be able to get rid of me easily, so they gave me a job as their PR person. I knew how to send out press releases and to whom, so it was a pleasure to start the next week. Other people arrived, were hired and the production company started work.

The taping began. We filmed in a large theatre in Hamilton, about 40 miles from Toronto. Part of my job was to meet the celebrity guests at the airport with a limo and take them to the theater. During that time I sat in the back seat with artists like Charles Aznavour and Michel Le Grand, Henry Mancini and all my idols. It was terrific to have one-to-one conversations with them.

One day in the office one of the stars cancelled at the last moment, so I took the opportunity to walk into my boss's office to give him a CD of Wendell. It was the perfect moment. He said he'd have to hear hm in person, so Wendell flew up to Toronto the next day, sang for both of them—only one verse—and they hired him. He was in the show. Mission accomplished. I still have the video of that show. Unfortunately, a few weeks later, Wendell suddenly died of a blood clot. It shocked all of us. At least he had appeared on prime time television singing with the greats.

Onward and Upwards. If only it was that easy!!

I was restless again, life was happening elsewhere and I wanted to be part of it. I knew I would never find another job like that in Toronto. It was a once in a lifetime show. I used to watch live Cabaret shows in the Imperial Room at the Royal York Hotel. Then they stopped. There were no other shows in Toronto except touring shows in the two large theatres downtown.

I flew back to New York. Wow! The energy was still there! You could smell it. I breathed it in as I took a taxi from the airport. I rented an apartment and settled in. It was near Central Park, so every day I walked in the Park. How many times I searched the *New York Times* classifieds.

Eventually I found a small ad looking for a personal assistant to a celebrity. When I phoned, the woman who answered wouldn't tell me who it was, but after some persuading she said it was for the actor Yul Brynner who was about to make his final American Tour, starring in *The King and I*. I got the job and saw more of America than I had dreamed of in the company of that wonderful show. I wrote about touring and working with Yul Brynner in my book, *Theatrical Feast of New York*.

# *Writing Books*

WHEN I WAS A STUDENT in London I was saving money so hard I would not spend anything on food.

I ate at the hostel. I rarely went to Lyons Corner House to buy a cup of tea or coffee; it was so awful anyway, but sometimes you needed to grab something on the way to class. So as I passed or read about all those wonderful restaurants in London, I hoped that one day I could afford to eat in them.

Rules, the Caprice, the Ivy, the Savoy Grill, Simpsons: oh, what heaven! Imagine: they serve the roast beef from a trolley with an enormous silver entree dish, with silver cover over it. At Simpsons in the Strand it takes two waiters to do it. Oh, how wonderful. Who will take me there?

Years later my husband did, luckily, and it triggered the idea for a book, *A Theatrical Feast of London*. I discovered a very old book in a second hand bookshop with personal recipes from famous actors. It was a godsend. Olivier, Gielgud, Noel Coward, Terence Rattigan had all signed the recipe below. So when the book came out it was reviewed in the *Times*.

A TV producer called me and wanted me on her show, to stand and watch their chef cooking Laurence Olivier's recipe. Then, when I wrote *A Theatrical Feast of New York* they asked me back, while he made a dish from Sardi's in New York. A barman set up a bar on the set, and proceeded to make Manhattans and Old Fashions on the show, so we all were terribly sloshed after the show. The Manhattans they serve at Sardi's are the best in New York and the most reasonable.

117

The King Cole Room at the St. Regis is the most expensive, something like $25 each at the last count.

Sardi was often seen walking around his restaurant, saying hello to regular customers. It was always a privilege to shake his hand. He really was a legend and when he died many famous actors wrote about how he had helped them when they were struggling, often running up a tab of hundreds of dollars to feed them.

Even today, he gives a discount to actors working on Broadway and on Wednesday matinee days he charges them a quarter of the price. Other stories about his generosity and love for actors have been written about in a number of books. I dedicated my book to him and to his grandson who is carrying on the business. It gives you a thrill when the Maitre'D recognizes you. My favorite dish is their onion soup, the best anywhere, including the long-gone Les Halles restaurants in Paris.

Later on, after visiting Cannes, the first visit being for the CBC, I loved the place so much I had to write about it.

*Positano*

---

## FINDING FRANCO ZEFFIRELLI

I WAS BACK IN HOBART with my brother, Roger just after Dad's funeral. Mother was in a nursing home not far away, so the two of us were trying to divide up the estate, as we knew that she would not be returning to the house, which would have to be sold. Anyone who has had to clear, sort and dispose of parent's possessions, knows how sad and devastating it can be. Even more so for us, because it didn't make sense for us to keep very much, because we both lived overseas. My brother had definite ideas of what should go where, what should be sold, and we began arguing, which was awful. I wanted to leave.

One morning I read in the newspaper that Franco Zeffirelli was going to be interviewed in New York at the Lincoln Center and that tickets were available on a first-come basis in about a week's time. It would be a chance to meet him and to hear about his new production at the Metroplitan Opera.

My brother was delighted to see me go. Mum was wrapped up in him, so my leaving was OK with her, so long as he remained and sorted everything out.

As every Opera and theatre buff knows, Zeffirelli stands for the best in producing anything Italian.

He was trained by the famous Visconti, who allowed him to watch how he directed, produced and of course, designed for the stage and film. I had followed his career since he discovered Dame Joan Sutherland at Covent Garden, after working with Maria Callas at the height of her career. He has the golden touch, and I will never forget hearing people weep in the Paris Theatre in New York when his film of *La Traviata* played there. This film is definitely my definitive production of that opera.

I managed to get a seat in the front row of the audience for his interview. At the question time afterwards, I was the first with a question. I was overcome with emotion and blurted out that I had just flown in from Australia so deserved to ask the first question, he looked at me with a smile that said:

"You mean you flew from there just to be here today?" The truth was I had.

Fifteen minutes later the members of the audience were invited to a Reception upstairs and a glass of wine. There was a huge crowd, but I looked over to see Zeffirelli was standing alone at the bar. I went up to him, he recognized me as the woman from Australia, we then had about 20 minutes' conversation before someone interrupted us. It may have been jet lag but after all the sadness I had just been through, to be talking to one of my heroes on a one-to-one basis was unreal.

My brother had wanted Dad to be cremated, which I hated the thought of, but after a long tearful day, he relented and Dad was buried next to his brother in a village churchyard in Campbell Town in Tasmania.

Suddenly I spoke to Zeffirelli about Maria Callas, asking him how did he feel when after she died, when before any of her friends knew, she was taken for cremation and her ashes scattered in the Aegean Sea. It was all done very quickly.

We talked about immortality, opera, composers, music. He spoke with such passion. I mentioned the documentary he had made about his filming of *Tosca* when he managed to use the actual locations for the plot, which takes place in Rome. Sometime later, it was wonderful to hear how the Met created two plaques in his honor on both sides of the stage, so the singers can see them as they enter and exit. He also describes in the documentary made about the life of Dame Joan Sutherland, laughing and retelling the first time he met her, and quickly found out she didn't like to be touched. He told her: "But I'm an Italian, I need to touch you, to hug you if necessary." So she quickly adapted.

His autobiography is full of wonderful anecdotes, including the fact that he was very nearly killed twice when he was a young soldier during World War II. The first time he was saved by a soldier who bent down for a cigarette, allowing him to dash behind a building and escape. Years later he made a film called *Tea with Mussolini,* which was about his harrowing time in Florence during the war. He was taken care of by a group of British women called the Scorpioni, played in the film by Maggie Smith, Judi Dench, Cher and Lily Tomlin.

A few years later while visiting Positano, I remembered reading that he owned a villa just outside town. That evening, after a few glasses of wine, I asked a taxi driver to drive us there. I was with my ever-patient husband who took along a bottle of Scotch as a present, and the taxi driver dropped us off by a small fence, by a long steep stone staircase.

I wondered if the maestro would remember me from the Lincoln Center. We started down the steps in the dark—they were rather steep—until we came to a gate and a bell. We rang the bell two or three times, but no answer. Finally we gave up; there were no lights and all was quiet, so we went back up the steps, and hailed a taxi back to the hotel.

Next morning, undaunted, I wanted to try again. So this time we walked to the villa, as it wasn't more than half a mile from the town. Again, we went down the steep steps to the little gate and rang the bell. I was apprehensive this time, and without the stimulus of the wine of the previous night, my confidence was wavering; we waited. A woman and a barking dog appeared this time. She spoke no English but my husband saved the day with his small knowledge of Italian. He told her that I had met the maestro in New York and was he at home? The woman then told us that he was in Rome and wouldn't be here for another week, then added that if we would like to come in and look around, she would be happy to escort us.

It was a glorious morning and I had brought my camera. Those were the days before digital ones.

I took photos of the three little villas which make up the estate, and the balcony terrace where all his sophisticated soirees were held with stars such as the Oliviers, Domingo, Callas, Sutherland and Leonard Bernstein. His favorite dog sitting on my lap was photographed too. It was a lovely visit, and later on we continued on down the steps to the beach below the villa with soft sand and a sheltered place to swim.

Back in London I excitedly went to pick up the photos from the photo shop. The film in the camera hadn't moved on after each shot, so the film was blank. I was devastated; there was nothing to record the day. Just one of life's disappointments. Thank goodness we have digital cameras now.

# New York Again

## THE ALGONQUIN HOTEL AND ROGER MOORE

BEFORE ROGER MOORE BECAME JAMES Bond, 007, he acted in a film series called *The Saint* on BBC.

He played almost the same elusive character, although probably without a gun. My brother worked as a cameraman on the show, and my sister-in-law, Jean, was delighted when she had her firstborn; she received a huge bouquet of flowers signed by Roger Moore. From then on we were all eager followers of his career.

Years later I had been presenting my "Spoken Word" programs at the Algonquin Hotel. I contacted the actor Barrie Ingham who had acted Shaw in my play *The Private Life of GBS*, with Rosemary Harris, to see if he could do another show for me the following Friday night. He phoned me from London to say he couldn't do it because he was appearing at the Albert Hall in a tribute to Trevor Nunn, who was leaving his position as head of the National Theatre of Great Britain.

A great number of actors were taking part in the tribute. Barrie Ingham was due to sing a duet with Roger Moore, singing "Brush Up Your Shakespeare." I thought that was pretty fantastic. Walking to the hotel a few nights later, who should I bump into outside the hotel waiting on the curb for a taxi, but Roger Moore!

I walked up to him and said: "Shouldn't you be with Barrie Ingham at the Albert Hall?" he answered. "No, that was last night." with a smile. Oh, what a smile!

I then introduced myself and said I was doing a program in the Oak Room that night about the poems of Noel Coward and would he like to come? He excused himself, saying he was going out to dinner but that he had worked with Coward. Then I said: "Well, if you would like to drop in after dinner"—obviously he was staying at the hotel—"perhaps you could say a few words about that experience."

The cab came and off he went. It was a brief exciting exchange.

We did the show. I had invited Hayley Mills to say a few words at the end of the program about Noel Coward; she had just finished when Roger and his wife made an entrance and the audience gasped.

The timing was perfect. I then introduced 007. He spoke about working with Coward, the master, and afterwards with his wife, graciously allowed people a photo op.

Kenneth Branagh was producing *The Play What I Wrote* at the time, and Roger was playing the Guest actor in the second act, as written in the script. I planned to see the matinee performance the next day. It turned out that it was Roger's last performance onstage. Half way through the second act, he fell onstage and passed out. The actor on stage thought he had taken a prat fall as the scene was rather like a vaudeville act, with Roger wearing a crinoline, but when he went up to Roger and said "Are you alright?" there was no answer. There was a deathly hush from the audience, and the curtain was lowered.

Shortly afterwards there was announcement that the play was ending early, because Roger had been taken ill; it was nearly at the end anyway.

We all heard the ambulance siren come then stop outside the stage door.

Later on we heard that he had had a mild heart attack and had a pacemaker put in. But he was out of danger.

I often wonder how Kenneth found a replacement for him at such short notice for the evening performance. The show must go on. It was a memorable moment to have met him outside the Algonquin. Then have him join us, just the the day before. Not every actor becomes a legend but I think Roger Moore is one of them. Kenneth will become one too. His early film *In the Bleak Mid Winter,* made years ago with Richard Briers, Joan Collins and Michael Maloney, about a small theatre company presenting Hamlet in a north country Church at Christmas, is a classic.

# Waiting For Noel Coward

ALTHOUGH I HAD SEEN A Coward play or two and was familiar with his songs, it wasn't until I had gone back to London after Yul Brynner's death, trying to write another play, when I picked up Sheridan Morley' official biography and read it. It was midwinter, raining and cold, black skies and windy nights.

I snuggled down under the blankets, totally carried away by the story of his life, rather as I had been years ago by Chopin's life. It was amazing. Page after page of what he was doing, writing, traveling, being witty, writing songs, and attending marvellous parties in the South of France. How creative, how energizing, how inspiring. So then I had a mission. To go to see his house and grave in Jamaica.

A short time later, after visiting the house, I wrote *Blue Harbour Revisited,* which continued my obsession with Coward. Then three more books, about his work. *Love from Shakespeare to Coward*, was the first one. Lady Redgrave acted in a one-act play called *Jamaican Interlude* which I based in Jamaica and we were fortunate enough to videotape shortly before she died. Later on, when working with the Algonquin Hotel, I based my newest play called *Waiting for Coward* at the hotel.

It is loosely based on Coward's play *Private Lives,* with the two couples meeting 30 years later while on holiday at the Algonquin. Later, the Actor's Guild produced it and we had a great time ironing out the quirks in the play. It is amazing what a group of professional actors can contribute when they are in rehearsals.

He loved to sail in ocean liners, so when I lecture on board ships, I usually include one lecture about him. Unfortunately, the younger generation does not know very much about him so I held regular sessions at the Theatre Museum, hiring a musician who could sing and play his songs. After any production I did there, I'd ask the young actors to stay and listen. It was the first time they had heard "Mad Dogs and Englishmen," "If Love Were All," and many other wonderful songs, including 'Why Must the Show Go On?'

Steve Ross, the Prince of Cabaret in Manhattan, specializes in Coward's songs. In fact, he was given Coward's green velvet evening jacket by the Noel Coward Society several years ago, and usually wears it when he is performing any Coward. He often generously invites guest artists to join him.

He joined me when I lectured at the Bruno Walter Auditorium at the Lincoln Center as well as inviting Tammy Grimes who sang "If Love Were All." She was Coward's leading lady on Broadway, as Judy Campbell was in London. There are so many anecdotes about Coward and Judy in the early days and Steve knows them all.

It was while Coward was having dinner at the Savoy Hotel, during the London Blitz, that a bomb hit the side of the hotel. The dining room was not affected but people were very shaken. Coward got up, went to the piano and sang some of his songs, then asked if there was anyone else in the room who could sing. A tall young woman stood up in a long white dress and walked to the stage. It was Judy Campbell and she sang "A Nightingale Sang in Berkeley Square." She made that her song, and sang it all through her life. Nobody can sing it like she could. Coward then cast her as his leading lady and they toured together around the UK.

Those days seemed so far away, but it was amazing that he kept going all through the Second World War. Fortunately his books are still in print, as well as his letters and diaries.

The younger generation might be interested to know that in fifty years time, most people will understand when someone says: "He was a very Noel Coward kind of person."

I continued presenting the programs at the Algonquin Hotel, finding wonderful actors at the same time. Ken Starrett, Executive Director for North America for the Noel Coward Society, helped me spread the word that we were doing Noel Coward's poems and many members joined us. Ken joined me to lecture on the Queen Mary 2 when the English Speaking Union of Palm Beach took a group to sail across to the UK.

Veronica James, an actress who is multi-talented, helped me not only by taking part, but with some of the casting details and paperwork. Her mother was a dancer who worked with Isadora Duncan in Paris and is was great to discover where the studio was with Veronica in Paris, several years later. Veronica has wonderful photos of herself dancing with her mother at a younger time.

When the Algonquin Hotel people decided to close the famous Oak Room, where all kinds of celebrities have sung, we were determined to close it out with the first musician ever to perform there, Steve Ross. I organized a dinner and an evening with Steve, once again, singing and playing, before the piano was removed the next day. Who knows what the future will bring?

# *Palm Beach*

I FIRST VISITED PALM BEACH on holiday. We were staying at a beach hotel several miles north of the resort. We drove our hired car down the famous Worth Avenue, the big shopping street, very similar to Rodeo Drive in Los Angeles. The same brand name fashion houses, Gucci, Chanel, Valentino and dozens more. Then we drove around the island. Palm Beach is an island roughly five miles long and less than five miles wide. All the beautiful mansions were surrounded by hedges and manicured gardens. It was rather like driving along the French Riviera, passing all those enormous villas and wondering what was going on inside. It was a few years later before I managed to see inside some of them.

At the time, we thought we could never meet anyone or get to know the residents, just as in Cannes or Nice, but then again you didn't have the language barrier you had over there. I once interviewed some women who lived on the Cote D'Azur for a magazine article, including the American wife of the crooked Mayor of Nice, when she was in her twenties, and she charmingly showed me her bedroom and private quarters in the manorial mansion. They were hounded after a scandal and fled to South America. But that is another story.

It was about 10 years later, when I was in New York, that I met a woman on the tennis courts who wanted me to drive down with her to Palm Beach, where she had a home. Evidently there were a great many New Yorkers who only went to Palm Beach for the winter months. She lived at the Palm Beach Tennis Club and said we could play tennis every day as well as go to other events.

I was suffering from a really bad cold that I had had for weeks and couldn't shake, when she called to invite me again. It was freezing outside. I was feeling miserable, so after a call to Canada to discuss all this, I was off. It was the beginning of a new life.

I felt the need of companionship and comfort of having someone who was interesting. She had been an actress, had married twice and had three children. Her father had been a Supreme Court Judge, and had left her a small fortune. However she had an enduring quality: she was so thrifty, and so amusing, I learnt a great deal from her. The first week we were there she took me on a tour of all the thrift shops in Palm Beach and West Palm Beach, as that is where she shopped. I was amazed. No Worth Avenue for her. She also darned her stockings and socks; watching her darning her pantyhose was a revelation.

Her refrigerator was full of foil-wrapped food, leftovers that she had taken as doggy bags from restaurants. Not from Private Clubs: they wouldn't allow it, but from regular places. And yet she was a millionaire several times over.

All these endearing habits went with her tremendous generosity But only close friends knew that side of her. She gave large parties and had a social standing in Palm Beach. She introduced me to all her friends. At Christmas time she would buy secondhand ties for the men in her life, and put each of them in a small jiffy bag, sealing them with a pretty bow.

Much has been written about Palm Beach. Most of the outside world has been told that it is a very wealthy enclave for blue-rinsed, old rich people who have canes, Cadillacs and crutches. A British documentary which was shown worldwide treated the place with contempt. Just a place for loud, very rich Americans. It is not until you stay here and find out what really goes on, do you have the knowledge to criticize. Yes, most of the residents are very rich, but most of the women spend their time and money on charitable organizations. Almost everyone works for a charity. The balls— The Heart Ball, the Red Cross Ball, the Salvation Army Ball—are to raise money for charity. Millions are given each year to these organizations. Social life is very regulated and there are several levels of society in the town.

Also it is a very cultural town. If anyone decides to retire to Florida, the best place to pick is Palm Beach because of a unique society: the Society of the Four Arts. It is like a mini-Lincoln Center in Florida. Remember, many of the residents are from New York and the northern cities, so they want to keep up with what is happening on the world stages.

The Society of the Four Arts has three buildings in a tropical garden in the centre of Palm Beach. Almost every day of the Season— from December to April—there are concerts, lectures, films, art exhibitions, classes and book groups. There is a library in a picturesque old building, an auditorium, an art gallery, classrooms, and a second concert hall in a beautiful tropical setting. International speakers and artists come from all over the world. To become a full member of the Society one has to be on the waiting list, which only clears when someone dies. You are also expected to donate a certain sum each year, in the thousands of dollars, to maintain your membership. One can join the Library for a modest fee and borrow the latest books, and DVDs.

I became friends with my namesake, Molly Charland—spelt with a C—and was invited to launch my books at a book launch there every year, as well as a lecture. The invitation was a great motivating factor in getting a book finished so it could be promoted in their annual catalogue of events.

The other great venue is the Kravis Center, a huge theatre across the bridge in West Palm Beach on the mainland, where they have three auditoriums. One very large one for touring Broadway shows, two for smaller producions, and an outside space. Recently they have added a Cabaret room and they invite artists from New York. There is also Cabaret Room in the famous old Colony Hotel at the top of Worth Avenue. I became the Food and Entertainment Editor for the Palm Beach Society Magazine six years ago, so I have the job of not only reviewing shows and cabaret, but the new restaurants that open as well.

The heavy social scene is usually between Christmas and Easter. The balls, parties and concerts take place at the celebrated Breakers Hotel, with tickets starting around $800 up to $1,500 per person. There are also many events at Mar-a-Lago, Donald Trump's mansion, which used to be Marjorie Merriweather Post's home. It is all rather over-the-top now, because the gift bags you receive on your way out contain items that have become ridiculous. Last year one gift bag contained a mini computer! It is not just cosmetics and perfume anymore.

There are three private clubs in town, or rather four, if you count the new Palm Beach Jewish Club where Madoff met and befriended most of his clients and made off with their money. Top of the list is the Everglades Club on Worth Avenue, where most of the old school set belong; they are very discriminating about new members, who have to be interviewed, proposed and seconded; then the Bath and Tennis Club, which is on the beach, and the Beach Club, also facing the beach, where many members have cabanas for the day, so they don't have to mingle with anyone and can dine outside on the patio. It is not necessary to become a member of a Club to enjoy the social life but there is a Social Register published each year which most Club members go by when issuing invitations.

Probably out of experience and past indiscretions, these Clubs keep close watch on member's behavior and have strict rules. Many people come to Palm Beach, including people seeking other people's fortunes.

West Palm Beach is a thriving newly-built city just across the bridge and growing rapidly. High rises are quickly going up and new restaurants open every other week. Real estate prices are going up, too. Ten years ago, there were incredible bargains, but you have to search for them now. It is still half the price of living in New York and other American cities, and the weather is wonderful.

I decided to rent a small auditorium and present the Spoken Word programs that I had done at the Algonquin Hotel in New York. I hired some local actors and they helped spread the word.

But it wasn't enough. I wrote another play *The Private Life of George Bernard Shaw,* and we had a reading of it at the Society of the Four Arts. I cast the 11 women that Shaw had had a relationship with, and just one man: Shaw himself. Fortunately there was a British actor living in the area and he played Shaw. Later on, when the British actor, Barrie Ingham—who had played Shaw for me at the Algonquin Hotel with Rosemary Harris—and his wife arrived in Palm Beach, I arranged for him to do some readings at the Chesterfield Hotel as a showcase. Molly Charland came and the folks from the Four Arts, who were very impressed; so after I had introduced them, he became a very popular teacher at the Society of the Four Arts for several years after that. We were all very shocked when he died in 2015. He had been a leading actor with the RSC in London and played leads with Judi Dench and Maggie Smith, as well as making films.

The place was a good place to write. There was no excuse. Plenty of time, glorious weather and interesting people. There are a great many Brits living there, including Churchill's granddaughter, artist Edwina Sands and Robert Spencer, second cousin to the late Princess Diana.

On the French Riviera, Cannes, is well known for its glamor, but they also have their famous world renowned Film Festival and in Venice, not only a Film Festival but their historic Carnival. It gives added interest to these places. So it would be good to have a similar attraction in Palm Beach we are trying.

For the past few years there has been a great deal of publicity about saving the Royal Poinciana Playhouse, and unless you know the history of this venue, you probably won't know that is featured in the history of legitimate theatre. International stars from all over the world played there, beginning in the early 1950s; the list of legendary stars is amazing. Christopher Plummer, who starred there, is a strong supporter of saving the theatre.

From legitimate theatre performers such as Helen Hayes, Carol Channing, Nathan Lane and other Broadway stars to movie stars such as Frank Sinatra, Bob Hope, Ginger Rogers and Claudette Colbert, all performed there. The adjoining dining room, the Celebrity Room, was a great draw, because it was convenient to have dinner before or after the performance.

Now we have the Kravis Centre supplying us with Broadway stars, international orchestras, ballet and opera companies and number-one road productions of Broadway shows.

However, there is still a need for a more intimate theatre, such as the Royal Poinciana, to produce shows that wouldn't fill the Kravis, but would be welcomed at a smaller theatre.

Reading the list of celebrities and performers who have worked here makes one wish that Palm Beach could be regarded as a theatre town once again. Performers love to work there during the winter season. Chris Plummer's former wife, Tammy Grimes, is still waiting!

She remembers the heyday of the Poinciana, as do many of the great stars.

John Gielgud loved coming here, and he gave poetry recitals at the Society of the Four Arts, Noel Coward swept into town, as did Douglas Fairbanks Jr. who settled here for a time, buying a house and inviting more theatre friends to join him. Others who performed at the theatre include Julie Harris, Michael Redgrave, Peter Ustinov, Charlton Heston, Hume Cronyn, Jessica Tandy, Mary Martin, Lucie Arnaz, June Allyson, Alan Alder, Rosemary Clooney, Joel Grey, Jerry Herman, Celeste Holm and of course, Palm Beach resident Arlene Dahl. One unexpected name is Dame Margot Fonteyn.

We also now have the fast growing Palm Beach Dramaworks, in West Palm Beach who have a lovely little theatre at the bottom of Clematis Street, and who are dedicated to producing serious plays and play readings. They present highly professional work, and have slowly built up a solid reputation of good theatre.

Which leaves us with the thought of a theatrical restaurant! As Food and Entertainment Editor here, I love to ponder this subject. I wonder if we could persuade Max Klimavicius to open a branch of Sardi's here, next door to the Royal Poinciana, or perhaps Joe Allen? All theatre towns have a theatre restaurant... where the performers all go to wind down, after a performance. There is a Joe Allens in London's West End theatre district (great food at reasonable prices) and another one just steps away from Broadway in New York...where you can often find Joe sitting at the bar.

It is an exciting thought, a theatrical restaurant, because it could be a wonderful venue with a possible cabaret room as well. But first we have to get the Royal Poinciana open again, and once more put Palm Beach on the international theatre map. British and US actors would be delighted to come here. Now if we could get one of them to open a restaurant, we'd be half way there. How about it Michael Caine?

Robert Russell runs the Royal Room at the Colony Hotel and he brings down performers such as Steve Ross, Tommy Tune, K.T. Sullivan, and many more from New York. It makes the town a first class cabaret venue.

# *Back To Tasmania*

THE LAST WORD MUST COME from home. The only thing I regret is that huge corporations have finally discovered Tasmania and we are now losing some of our legacy to high commerce. I suddenly thought of all the writers who have written about the old days and besides my father, made history there.

Nan Chauncy is a name most Tasmanian writers know well. My father knew her well, and as a child I remember our family driving to see her in her cottage just outside the village called Bagdad.

After her death, the cottage and gardens were opened as a Nature Reserve.

Originally from England, she settled in Tasmania after working in various parts of the world, including teaching in Denmark. She wrote children's books that mostly featured stories of the bush, nature, birds and exciting country adventures. She also organized the Girl Scouts and became a leader for further Scout packs across the Island. We would have afternoon tea with her and her husband, and it was fascinating to talk about the various birds and animals she had seen on her country walks. She went on to win all kinds of awards, and several films were made of her books, one of which won at the Venice Film Festival for Best Children's Film.

I remember how down to earth she was, and how much she loved writing about the island. My memory of Dad's friends were how they were still discovering and exploring the different flora and fauna of the island. Their spiritual life was bound up by their love of the land.

Since leaving Tasmania I have given a great deal of thought about where writers work the best. If we do have some kind of history in our souls, or believe in reincarnation, it seems to explain why most of us know when and where we are contented. Reading about my grandfather, even going back to my great grandfather's brother, who left Tasmania, went to England, studied to be a doctor, but then came back to New Norfolk and practiced there for the rest of his life. In those days, traveling back and forth took months, and in very primitive ships, battling storms and the heat of the tropics.

Maybe because Dad's ancestors originally come from Normandy, my brother, Roger lived there for the last 20 years of his life and he loved it. It seems strange that he never wanted to return to Tasmania, but felt at home in Normandy. Even though he was lonely at times, he said that the sky was larger there than anywhere else, and the landscape was more verdant and pleasing.

He did return when Dad died, and arranged that he be buried in Campbell Town, a country town in the Midlands, where we laid Mum to rest as well. They were both devoted to each other and I think their mutual love of nature and the pursuit of preserving the uniqueness of the island's beauty was their life's work.

Elizabeth Sharland
www.sharland.com

ELIZABETH SHARLAND IS AN ACTRESS, producer, playwright and novelist, best-known for her informative and entertaining non-fiction books about theatre - and for her popular and long-running show Love From Shakespeare to Coward, an anthology of plays poems, letters and diaries around the theme of love, based on six years in the West End using over 200 actors in showcases.

She has lectured at the Harvard Club in New York, as well as the University Club, the National Arts Club, the Players Club and the Lincoln Center for the Performing Arts. In London, she has lectured at the National Portrait Gallery and the Concert Artistes Association.

Her book Behind the Doors of Notorious Covent Garden is a colourful guide to the cultural heart of London, including a history of its many theatres and restaurants. Passionate Pilgrimages is a fascinating look at the homes and studios of legendary composers, artists and writers across Europe, while her other books include A Theatrical Feast: Sugar and Spice in London's Theatreland, Love From Shakespeare to Coward and The British on Broadway.

Elizabeth is now the Food and Entertainment Editor of the Palm Beach Society Magazine, reviewing restaurants and theatres in Palm Beach, Florida. She trained at the Guildhall School of Music and Drama and joined the Old Vic Company to tour Australia. She has had plays produced in London and New York, formed an English-speaking theatre company in Paris, worked for Yul Brynner on Broadway, and also lectures regularly on the Queen Mary 2, between London and New York. She has one son, and travels frequently between Europe and America.

Printed in the United States
By Bookmasters